DAN WALDORF

is a research sociologist at Scientific Analysis Corporation in San Francisco and has written extensively about drug treatment programs in New York. Before his interest in drug problems, he lived in and wrote about an English New Town, worked with an action program for the aging, did a planning study in New York City, and has been at one time or another a blacksmith, a rigger in a shipyard, a jazz disc jockey, and a salesman.

DAN WALDORF

Careers in Dope

SCENARIO FOR AN ADDICT: "Everything I do is completely original—I made it up when I was a little kid."

> Claes Oldenburg (From the preface to the catalogue of his Moderna Musett exhibition, Stockholm 1966)

SCENARIO FOR A SQUARE: "The closer we get to the center of the problem, the closer we come to the dilemma of drug use: do people use drugs, or do drugs use people? We like to say that the first is true; we act as if the second were. At the center of the addict is the answer; perhaps for our peace of mind, it is better not to inquire too closely."

> Peter Laurie (From Drugs: Medical, Psychological, and Social Facts)

A SPECTRUM BOOK

PRENTICE-HALL, INC · ENGLEWOOD CLIFFS, NEW JERSEY

Library of Congress Cataloging in Publication Data

WALDORF, DAN.
    Careers in dope.

    (A Spectrum Book)
    Bibliography: p.
    1. Heroin. 2. Narcotic addicts—New York (City)
3. Drug abuse—Treatment—New York (City) I. Title.
[DNLM: 1. Diacetyimorphine. 2. Drug addiction.
3. Life style. 4. Social problems. WM 288 W166c
1973]
HV5822.H4W34   362.2′93′097471   72-13655
ISBN 0-13-114660-2
ISBN 0-13-114652-1 (pbk)

10 9 8 7 6 5 4 3 2 1

PRENTICE-HALL INTERNATIONAL, INC. (London)
PRENTICE-HALL OF AUSTRALIA, PTY. LTD. (Sydney)
PRENTICE-HALL OF CANADA, LTD. (Toronto)
PRENTICE-HALL OF INDIA PRIVATE LIMITED (New Delhi)
PRENTICE-HALL OF JAPAN, INC. (Tokyo)

Contents

Introduction

Let me say at the onset that I believe that heroin addiction is a serious social problem in the United States, particularly in New York City, and that we are experiencing a definite epidemic of heroin use. Both problem and epidemic are, however, of our own making; they are very much "made in America." We are not by any means the only country in the world that has large numbers of addicts—addicts seem to be particularly endemic to capitalist countries[1]—but as a nation we have made more fuss, spent more money, enacted more repressive laws, and experienced less success in controlling heroin addiction than any country in recent history.

Perhaps we made our principal mistake in 1914, at the time of the passage of the Harrison Act, with our assumption that opiates were evil and pernicious drugs. I say assumption, because at that time we knew very little about opiates. We know much more now: opiates are neither evil nor pernicious. The research has been in a long time; alcohol, which we accept and even encourage, is much more dangerous to life and health than opiates ever were. Opiates *do not* cause people to commit violent crimes, rape, or sexual of-

---

1. A comparative study of data from the United Nations indicates that Hong Kong, Japan, the Republic of Korea, Canada, the Federal Republic of Germany, India, Burma, and Iran have the largest numbers of heroin addicts; see Susan I. Kim, *Narcotic Addiction: A Comparative Study of Eight Countries,* Columbia University, Bureau of Applied Social Research, 1968.

fenses. Opiates *do not* of themselves cause any major physical or mental deterioration.

Opiates *do* cause physical dependence. They *do* cause most persons who use them, but not all, to abandon productive activities; most certainly opiate addicts lay around and sleep a good deal. They are not by any stretch of the imagination achievers in the traditional Protestant-ethic sense. Opiate use *does* create certain strains in day-to-day family relations that probably have negative effects on those who live around a user.

Addicts in the United States *do* die at a higher rate than non-addicts in comparable age groups; overdose is the major cause of these deaths. Addicts *do* contract serum hepatitis and demontrate a stellar disregard for their health. Addicts under our present system of control *do* commit innumerable criminal acts in search of money to buy the drugs they need. Addicts *do* manipulate and exploit people in unmerciful ways; nearly everyone they meet is a potential victim of whatever ruse or scheme they can think of to raise money. But these hazards and the criminal activities of addicts are not the direct result of the drugs they use; they are, rather, the result of the social conditions surrounding its use in the United States.

Another of our monumental mistakes in controlling opiate use was to give the responsibility for control to law-enforcement agencies. When federal and state legislation criminalized the addict we drove him underground and made a pariah out of him. This criminalization has caused addicts to band together in a primitive defense of themselves and has set them at odds with the values and goals of society. If they were not criminal when they began to use opiates they soon became criminal—because repressive laws forced them to. Contrary to the almost fictitious reports of the old Federal Bureau of Narcotics, law-enforcement efforts have had no discernible effects upon the flow of heroin into the United States. In some respects cynical critics of our drug policies are correct in their belief that law-enforcement agencies are too involved in drugs—in making money in various ways and in building careers—ever to control the inflow of heroin. In some areas of New York City, notably Central Harlem, Bedford-Stuyvesant, and the South Bronx, heroin is so plentiful (it is on nearly every street) that it would seem to be there with the knowledge and sanction of the police; it is, in effect, legal. Testimony before the Knapp Commission on police corruption in New York City in 1971 indicated that the police have been intricately involved with the sale of heroin and other drugs and have been more often the agents of spreading drug abuse than its controllers.

We, as a nation, have created our own problems by making monsters out of addicts. It is society's laws and society's behavior toward the addict that have created so many criminals out of addicts, so many persons who are obviously at odds with society. Heroin did not do it, addicts did not do it; society did it, and we delude ourselves if we think that the problem lodges with addicts and not with ourselves and society.

This is all prelude to the principal point that I wish to make in this introduction—that this book will not deal with the horrors of drug abuse. There will be no nightmare stories about drug users here. Rather it will be a book about the addict and his life at the hands of society. There are already too many books, too many articles that assume the established point of view; I do not wish to do that. I want to describe the life of the addict and his career in dope —how he begins to use heroin and becomes addicted; how he supports himself and raises money to support his need; how he suffers at the hands of society; how he gets arrested and goes to jail or for treatment; and, for a few, how he gives up heroin use and overcomes the pariah status to which society has demoted him.

My approach is not particularly new or unique. It is known by all of those who have an interest in people on the other side, those outside the pale, with what used to be known as the low life. This is the world of novelists such as Charles Dickens, Fyodor Dostoevsky, Jean Genêt, Jerzy Kozinski, Nelson Algren, John Rechy, William Burroughs, and others. Sociology has its own men of the black world; Edwin Sutherland's study of the professional thief was the precursor of Howard Becker, Ned Polsky, Irving Goffman, Alfred Lindesmith, and Herbert Blummer—who form something of a school within sociology. Essentially, the approach of these sociologists and novelists is to disregard the customary and easily assumed moralistic, established position toward deviance and to concentrate their efforts and perceptions on the meanings of men's actions to themselves, not to society. This is not done in any superficial psychological sense; they do not attempt to look for events or patterns of events in the individuals' lives to account for their deviant behavior. Rather, they look at the actor and his actions within a larger sphere —as a philosophy, as a way of life, as a career, as a way to deal with an environment or society that is hostile to large classes of people. They do not set out to seek "causes" of deviance or criminality (this has been an overriding concern with almost everyone who writes about addiction), but they attempt to describe the world of the deviant as he or she lives in it. They attempt to get into the world or get into the head of the other person, believing that this is where genuine understanding will come from.

This approach has not been utilized as it might to study drug abuse or addiction. Alfred Lindesmith used it in his first work, *Opiate Addiction*; so did Howard Becker in his seminal study of beginning marijuana use[2] and his tape recording of the biography of a female addict.[3] Addicts have most assuredly an advantage in taking this approach, and novels and biographies by addicts provide, despite the voluminous research literature on addiction, the most reliable descriptions of the heroin addict's life. There is nothing in the literature of addiction that can compare with the biography of Janet Clark[3] or with the writings of Alexander Trocchi, William Burroughs and Piri Thomas.[4] They are, however, writers of the first rank, as is obvious when you compare their work with the trite and trivial descriptions found in most of the writing about drug use and addiction.

I am by no means an addict, only an occasional drug user (alcohol and marijuana), so I do not speak from any extensive direct, personal experience with heroin or addiction, but I have met, listened to, talked to, and become friends with many addicts during the course of this study and its writing and feel that I have some understanding of their lives. You do not have to be an addict to write about addiction meaningfully. It certainly helps to write from direct experience, as Burroughs, Trocchi, and Thomas have shown, but you do not have to have a condition to know something about it.

What I speak from is a certain sympathy and understanding of the addict and his situation vis-à-vis American society, coupled with objective data about the processes of his life. I most assuredly have a bias in favor of the addict, but the data used are objective; they were gathered and analyzed according to accepted standards of methodology at a university that has prided itself on its methodological accomplishments. I have, however, interpreted these data according to the approach described earlier, and that approach is definitely sympathetic.

2. Howard Becker, "Becoming a Marijuana User," *Outsiders* (New York: The Free Press, 1963).

3. Helen MacGill Hughes (ed.), *The Fantastic Lodge* (Greenwich, Conn.: Fawcett World Library, Premier Books, 1971).

4. See the bibliography for books by Trocchi, Burroughs, and Thomas.

THE OBJECTIVE DATA

Data and information for this book come from several sources. The primary data come from life-history interviews with 422 men, all heroin users, who were interviewed in five different treatment facilities located in New York State. The analyses of these life-history data make up six chapters of this book. Similarly, 147 women heroin users were interviewed at Manhattan Rehabilitation Center, one of the New York State civil commitment facilities, at two periods: in 1968, 95 women were interviewed, and in 1969 there were an additional 52 interviews. The project also interviewed 116 patients from the Harlem Hospital Methadone Maintenance Program (analyzed in chapter 7) and 31 persons[5] from a variety of other programs and sources to study the processes and events that lead them to abstain from heroin use for long periods of time. This last study is described in chapter 9, "Rock Bottom."

The second source of data was periodic record checks on the progress made in the various programs by all the persons we interviewed. These were made at varying times for the three different programs involved (the New York State Civil Commitment Program, New York City's Phoenix Houses, and the Harlem Hospital Methadone Maintenance Program) and were used to assess and evaluate the effectiveness of the respective programs. These evaluations appear in chapters 6 and 7.

These quantitative data were supplemented by more than 1,000 field reports, which deal principally with the various treatment facilities that we were evaluating but also include some aspects of the life histories of many of the persons we talked to. The qualitative data from these field reports are used in a number of ways and are woven in and out of the quantitative data to illustrate and elaborate them.

THE MALE SAMPLE

As the analysis of the male sample makes up the bulk of the book I would like to begin with a brief description of that sample.

5. This was a nonrandom sample.

Each of the other samples is described within the text of the chapter that it forms.

The male addicts in the five facilities sampled were very much urban and working-class in character. The majority were raised within New York City; two out of three (68%) reported that they were living in that city when they were five years old, three out of four (74%) lived there when they were ten years old, and more than four out of five (84%) lived there during the year previous to their stay in treatment. Of the five boroughs of New York City Manhattan contributed the highest percentage, followed by the Bronx and Brooklyn. Black and Puerto Rican ghettoes such as Central and East Harlem, South Bronx, Bedford-Stuyvesant, and Williamsburg were well represented.

Three out of four (75%) reported coming from homes where the head of the household had held a semiskilled, skilled, or unskilled job, and half of those (37% of the total sample) were themselves in unskilled or semiskilled occupations. Only a few came from middle-class homes and most of these were white.

Blacks showed up more often in the samples than Puerto Ricans and whites. More than two out of every five persons (44%) were black, with another 30% Puerto Rican and almost a quarter (24%) white. This ethnic breakdown is similar to that found by the New York City Health Department's Narcotic Registry. Of the 52,-000 heroin abusers reported to that registry up to 1968 (the Registry started recording names and other data in 1964), nearly half were black (48%), with a quarter Puerto Rican (24%) and a quarter white (24%). We sampled fewer black addicts and more Puerto Ricans, but in general our sample is similar in ethnicity to the best estimates of the population of New York addicts.

Persons in our sample were young; the average age was 25 years, but the median (the point at which half of the 422 men were younger and half were older) was 23 years. If they were young, they were by no means inexperienced with heroin—the average length of use was five years, with a range of from one month to 32 years. The man who had used heroin and other opiates for 32 years was a hardy and robust Chinese, who began the use of opiates in Hong Kong and came to the United States at the end of World War II.

While all of the men had used heroin, not all considered themselves to be addicted. More than one out of every four (28%) *did not* consider himself an addict, but most of these persons thought they were in danger of addiction; only a minority (7%) were adamant in reporting that they were neither addicted nor in danger of addiction. We did not attempt to establish any objective means of determining addiction (physical addiction is relatively difficult to determine while a person is using heroin—the best method is to isolate the individual and observe the development of withdrawal symptoms—and impossible when persons are abstinent in treatment facilities), so these self-reports are our only data. I believe, however, that the user more than anyone should know whether or not he is addicted. He is the one who experiences withdrawal symptoms; if he recognizes them and makes the association with his heroin use, then he should know if he is addicted or not. I would expect that many of those who denied addiction were *not* actually physically addicted. This was possible because most of the persons in our samples were committed to treatment under New York State civil commitment laws (89%), and actual physical addiction is not a necessary condition for that commitment.[6] Often persons who were suspected of being only in danger of addiction were committed. Many of the youngest men in the sample fit into this category. These were usually instances where the parents had discovered the heroin use of their offspring and had had them committed to "treatment" under a voluntary section of the state commitment law.

The majority of the men were raised in Catholic families, and more than half (54%) said that they were raised in that religion. The Protestants were next, with more than a third of the men (37%). At 7%, Jews were only a small percentage of the samples. Surprisingly, religion did not figure in any of the analyses of the major findings of the study; I mention it here only because I think it ought to be included.

The male heroin user is not what one would consider marriageable; he is definitely not, in the parlance of a security conscious mother, a "good catch." The maintenance of a heroin habit is, perhaps, too demanding to allow him to assume the financial and emotional responsibilities of marriage. More than two-thirds (68%) reported that they were single and had never been married, while only 16% reported that they were married at the time of the interview. This naturally varied with age; the older the addict, the less likely

6. This is legal under numerous state commitment laws in the United States and is common practice in both New York and California. All of the persons in our samples who were not committed to treatment were in Phoenix Houses, while all the persons in the other facilities were committed.

he was to report that he was single. But even the oldest group had
a large percentage of persons who had never married; 39% of those
over 26 said they were single, compared to 65% of those from 21 to
26 and 93% of those under 21.

This did not always, however, preclude living relationships
with women, because nearly a third (32%) of those who said they
were single and had never been married told interviewers that they
had at some time maintained a household with a lover or a common-
law wife. Certainly many of these relationships were of the same
order as a marriage, and while addicts as a group do not marry
formally as often as the nonaddict population does, there are many
who do form consensual relationships with women.

Women addicts are another thing altogether; they are far more
apt to be married than are the males. Both the ratio of male to
female addicts and the general economics of hustling to maintain a
habit cause women addicts to be much more in demand than men,
and as a consequence many more females than males are married
or have lovers. (For a more detailed discussion, see chapter 10,
"Women Versus Men.")

Generally, the men of the samples were obvious products of
poverty, the particular poverty of the minority ghettoes of New
York. Heroin use and addiction are ubiquitous in the poor neighborhoods of New York and have been since the early 1950s. This is
especially true in the minority ghettoes. Heroin is seemingly every-
where in black and Puerto Rican ghettoes, and young people growing up there are aware of it from an early age. They know of heroin
and addicts through close scrutiny—they see the endless trade of
money for white powder, they see the user nod on the front stoop,
they watch him "get off" in the communal bathroom down the hall,
they observe his theft of the family TV set. The wonder of New
York ghettoes is not that so many become users and addicts to this
amazing, powerful drug that offers relief from an oppressive environment, but that the majority somehow, someway resist it.

[1]

Addiction
as a Career

The physiological dependence created by heroin and the tendency of users to develop tolerances to it cause most heroin addicts to devote considerable time and effort to the search for the drug. Heroin becomes an organizing force in the life of an addict. It gives his life a precise and regular structure; while he is addicted he must take the drug at regular intervals—every day, seven days a week, with no holidays or weekends off. The consequences of a failure to meet the physical need for heroin are immediate—the addict becomes anxious and irritable and starts to experience an array of withdrawal symptoms. These "changes" and symptoms are a constant reminder that he must consider and support his habit.

A heroin habit is a real thing to an addict; he seems to be possessed by it. It is experienced as both a physical and a psychological entity, experienced at once in his body and in his head.[1] Withdrawal symptoms testify to the addict's physical dependence, and the recurrent tendency to relapse after both voluntary and involuntary abstinence would seem to demonstrate to him both heroin's physical and its psychological characteristics.

The actual process of addiction requires certain minimal knowledge and skills. The beginning addict must learn how to use the drug efficiently, how to buy and sell it, how best to administer it,

1. See Mac Proctor's interesting article "The Habit," in *The International Journal of the Addictions*, Vol. 6, no. 1 (1971).

9

and how to avoid detection by the police and other authorities. It also requires certain associations with other users or addicts to get the drug and to learn the necessary skills.

Contrary to popular belief, addicts are not inactive, lazy people. While high they *do* lie around, sleep, and nod a good deal, but addicts are *not* always high. Many New York addicts *do* seem to hang out a good deal, but that is usually for the specific purpose of purchasing drugs. While seeking money for drugs they are often active and resourceful hustlers—buying and selling large and small supplies of drugs, making a round of thefts and selling their booty, running an imaginative con or turning steady tricks as a prostitute.

The need for heroin requires an active life. The addict *may* be, as psychologists have claimed, depressed,[2] he may be psychopathic,[3] and he may use drugs to escape some reality in his life,[4] but he is active in pursuit of a demanding life that requires considerable skill and ability to sustain. Addiction is *not* some aberrant, part-time leisure activity that one indulges in from time to time but that never engages one's life. On the contrary, addiction does engage the addict in an active life that has a precise purpose and satisfies a specific physical need. Whatever the individual's motives for using heroin or the ways in which a specific addict approaches his heroin use, he most certainly experiences an absorbing or engrossing drive, lives an active life, and is very much part of a social group.

Addiction, as it is engrossing and requires certain skills and abilities, can also be seen as a life style or career. By "career" I do not mean the term as it is used to describe the professional activities of a surgeon, a business executive, or an actress but in a broad sociological sense. A career in this sense ". . . is not a thing that can be brilliant or disappointing; it can no more be a success than a failure."[5] It is an activity or sequence of activities with a natural history that is seen without particular regard to high or low points but rather to the changes over time that are common to the participants. In this sense careers such as pool hustler, felon, hippie, mental pa-

2. S. Rado, "Fighting Narcotic Bondage and Other Forms of Narcotic Disorders," *Comprehensive Psychiatry*, Vol. 4, no. 3 (1963); Sidney Weissman, "The Significance of Diagnosis in Treatment of Narcotic Addicts," *The International Journal of the Addictions*, Vol. 5, no. 4 (1970).

3. H. E. Hill, C. A. Haertzen, and R. Glaser, "Personality Characteristics of Narcotic Addicts as Indicated by the MMPI," *Journal of General Psychology*, Vol. 62 (1960).

4. Isidor Chein, Donald L. Gerard, Robert S. Lee, and Eva Rosenberg, *The Road to H* (New York: Basic Books, Inc., 1964).

5. Erving Goffman, *Asylums* (Garden City, N.Y.: Doubleday & Company, Inc., 1961).

tient, and alcoholic can be approached in the same way as those of lawyer, doctor, businessman, pop star, and so forth. And so the career of the heroin addict, which I will pursue through his initiation, work life, stays in jail and in treatment, cycles of abstinence and relapse, and, for a few, ex-addict life.

INITIATION TO HEROIN

Most persons who use heroin have some firsthand experience with other users or addicts before they actually use it themselves. In fact, most working-class persons who live in New York ghettoes know a good deal about heroin and addicts and usually speak very disparagingly of both. Very few people approach heroin use with the idea of becoming an addict. The initial use of heroin is usually for its pharmacological effect, for the high that is offered and expected. It is only one of several drugs that the novice is experimenting with before actual heroin use; the others are usually marijuana and alcohol (for working-class persons—for the middle classes add LSD, amphetamines, and barbiturates). It is usually this experimentation that sets the stage for—creates an interest and curiosity in—the use of heroin and other drugs.

Beginning heroin use nearly always arises out of some social situation in which a friend or an acquaintance offers the novice a new and exciting experience—heroin. This can occur at a dance, at a party, on a street corner, in a bar, or most anywhere. Most persons use it the first time either to satisfy a certain intellectual curiosity generated by their earlier experimentation or to gain acceptance among a group of peers.

Unlike marijuana, most persons enjoy their first use of heroin and experience the euphoria it offers on their first time. But not everyone does; some have to learn how to use it. Those who must wait or learn to use it have to find out the proper dosage, to overcome the initial feelings of nausea, and to let themselves enjoy its particular high.

In many respects heroin is, as addicts say, the "king of drugs." It offers most of those who use it their best drug experience, the best of highs, without too many negative side effects. The strong analgesic properties of the drug allay most of the anxiety and tension the user may experience and cause him to feel detached from physical pain and bodily symptoms. This disassociation from pain and anxiety causes the user to feel more the master of fate than its victim; the user becomes, in the words of Alexander Trocchi, *inviolable*. The worst of the negative effects of heroin is the physical dependence it causes, but this is considerable in a society that disparages and criminalizes the user.

BECOMING A USER

Steady, unbroken use can lead to physical dependence in a relatively short time (a week or two, depending upon the dosage and frequency of use), but most persons are more casual and incidental in the beginning. As with the first use, social situations are the focus for these continuing incidents, and the users are nearly always dependent upon other persons to get the drug and teach them its use.

Any continued casual use necessitates information, some dependable source or sources, and, perhaps, paraphernalia ("works"). This is where other users or addicts come to influence the life of the experimenter. Other users usually provide the needed information (where to "cop" or "score," how to make a "set of works") and skills (how to "skin pop" subcutaneously or inject the drug intravenously) for continuing use.

On a more symbolic level the association also gives the initiate a social identity—heroin user. Heroin use is not by any means so widespread or extensive that it is not unusual to have used heroin. The user's experience of heroin and his association with other users allow him to feel something special and to relish having experienced something that most people have not. It allows him to stand apart from society, to be different. It often gives him status among his peers. There may be other gains from association with users as well—the opportunity to speak with others like himself, to talk about and assess their drug experiences, the opportunity to form friendships on a basis of shared experience. The user may find that he enjoys these relationships, and they in turn reinforce his use of heroin.

THE ADDICT-HUSTLER

Protracted casual heroin use usually culminates in physical addiction. Some persons phase out of heroin use (move out of an area of use or lose their original sources) after an initial experimental period, but most persons who continue to use heroin for any long period will become addicted. The pattern for New York addicts is an apprenticeship of from 6 to 12 months.

Increasing tolerances for heroin and physical addiction (or its realization), force most users into hustling to support their need. Heroin is expensive and most users are young and ill-equipped— without education or specific work experience—to support by any legal means an escalating habit that must be attended to every day. Most persons are forced to utilize whatever resources, skills, and ingenuity they have. Women and girls have an advantage in this regard: they have a ready commodity for which there is demand— their bodies. Prostitution is at once a convenient, easy, and profitable profession for the female addict.

Men, on the other hand, are usually forced by their addiction to develop a variety of hustles until they attain some special skill or specialization. Male addicts usually participate in an array of hustling activities—one day stealing from family or friends; the next day out of parked cars; the next, stores; the next, from old people on the street. The booty can range from the family TV set to car radios, from stolen meat to small or large amounts of cash.

Regular hustling seems to foster the development of a specific sensitivity. The hustler learns in a short time how to size up people and situations precisely and quickly—to recognize persons who are vulnerable to theft and situations that can bring him easy cash or materials that can be bartered for money. New York addicts learn very quickly how to break into cars and dismantle radios; how with a team of two one can distract a store clerk at one end of the store while the second robs the other end; how to enter an apartment or house through a door or window, assess the goods of value, and walk out with them—often right in front of a door man. But these are only the mechanics of the hustle; more subtle are the abilities to recognize undercover police and to assess the vulnerability of an individual or a situation. The skilled addict-burglar can cruise down a street, spot the "easy apartments," recognize the houses where the occupants are away, and assess the security systems of stores and business offices. The skilled street prostitute knows exactly whom to encourage or discourage, whom to avoid at all costs.

THE VICTIMS, THE COMMUNITY, AND THE POLICE

Regular hustling forces the creation of new relationships in the life of the addict: those between the hustler and his victims, the community that buys and receives his booty, and the police. First victims are usually family and friends. Upon initial addiction the user approaches them with a variety of money-raising appeals ("I'm sick, I need money for drugs") and ruses ("I need money to buy 'dollies' [methadone] in order to get clean"). These are repeated until the user's credit is exhausted, until he has burned his bridges, and the family and friends resist the requests. When this happens the male user resorts to stealing money and easily redeemable objects, justifying these thefts on the basis of his need—he needs drugs and has to have money to buy them.

The next victims are neighbors and the local community. Individuals and families of the addict's own community are mugged or burgled; small businesses and shops are boosted and robbed on a regular basis. The hustler goes to his own community first because that is the one he knows the best. This may also include the community of heroin users; other users are often hustled and burned like the nonuser. Addicts often take the money of strangers and friends alike, sell "short" and "overcut" bags to the unsuspecting, and steal drugs and money from each other.

One cannot, however, continue to steal from one's own community and get away with it for very long. As the hustler exhausts his own community or acquires more skill or confidence, he moves into neighborhoods where he is not known. Usually this movement is to a more prosperous area. Burglars shift their activities to middle-class apartment houses whose occupants work during the day or to large, but vulnerable, businesses downtown; rip-off thieves (muggers) move to wealthier, dark, residential streets; shoplifters go downtown to boost the large department stores; con men move into the rich Eastside bars. In this way the rich and middle classes become part of the economic system of the addict.

At the same time, the local community of the addict can benefit from his hustling. He begins his stealing from his local community, but he also sells his booty to them. Innumerable items—color TV sets, high-fidelity equipment, clothing, jewelry, food, and so forth—are resold to the community at a fraction of their original cost. The purchase of stolen goods is a regular activity in the poor areas in which most addicts live. Often addicts will have a regular round of customers, and customers often place orders for things that they want. In this respect there is a specific and recurrent cooperation of the addict community with the nonaddict community. The addict gets money for drugs, and the nonaddict, material objects that he might otherwise be unable to afford. This complicity results in an obvious vested interest on the part of the nonaddict community to maintain the addict in his role as a hustler entrepreneur.

Another important relationship of the addict is his close and continuing one with the police. More and more of the efforts of law-enforcement agencies center around the addict and his drug seeking. The problem of addiction in New York has become synonymous with the law-and-order issue; addicts are blamed wholesale for most of the crime in the city. They are most certainly responsible for a good deal of it, but not as much as is attributed to them.

The day-to-day relationships of addicts and narcotics police are rather like that of cat and mouse. The police, playing the cat, garner all the advantage. They assume, and society gives them, a moral superiority. Society, bewildered and frightened by addicts, has given law-enforcement agencies nearly free rein in dealing with them. There have been stiffer and stiffer sentences for possession and sale of drugs and, more recently, the passage of the federal no-knock law, giving the police even more power to enter and search.

Comfortable in their moral superiority, narcotics police in New York rip and roar through drug neighborhoods (it is not surprising that these are minority neighborhoods as well) stopping to frisk, search, or coerce people on the slightest pretext. Only one out of every two drug arrests in New York results in conviction, and for every arrest there must be several shakedowns or threatened shakedowns.

Police also use addicts regularly as informers, turning one addict against another. The payoff for the police are felony arrests; for the addict-informer it is drugs and a certain temporary immunity from arrest. As a matter of practice, New York narcotics police regularly hold back part of the heroin that is confiscated in large-scale arrests to use it as pay for informers.

Addict-sellers are also a source of bribe money. Many large sellers in New York operate openly without fear of arrest because they make regular payments to the local police precinct (from precinct captains to foot patrolmen) which, in turn, guarantees immunity. Smaller fry, such as ounce dealers, often pay arresting officers bribes to lower the charges or to botch the charges in such a way that reasonably clever lawyers can get them dropped or dismissed. In this way narcotics has become a major source of corruption in the New York police force.

It is hardly surprising that New York's top narcotics detective was charged and dismissed from the force for drug importation—the narcotics units of both city and federal governments in New York

have been centers of continual scandal in recent years. Detectives of
the city's narcotic units are transferred regularly in an effort to slow
or impede corruption, but there is so much money involved in
heroin sales that it is a rare cop who is not involved in some bribery.

The addict in this relationship seems to appreciate the heightened excitement that the police chase offers. Society's heavy and
abiding concern and the flurry of police activity are often interpreted by the addict as evidence of heroin's importance and power.
The reasoning is often thus: "If heroin is *not* such an important
and powerful drug, why is society so concerned about it? They enact
all these laws and put us in jail because they themselves are afraid
of it." Being illegal makes the drug attractive in the eyes of many,
and the cat-and-mouse game with the police makes drug seeking by
the addict an exciting and dramatic activity. Like the Westerns and
the courtroom and medical dramas on TV, where every drama, every
installment, is a cliff hanger, the addict-hustler is threatened by detection and jail every day. This is, I am sure, the basis for the
addict's belief that he is leading a far more different and exciting
life than the square. It is not unlike the excitement that surrounded
alcohol and speak-easies during the era of prohibition, when the
surreptitious nature of its use created a certain aura and impetus
for its continuation. Much of the "excitement" of the addict's life
comes from these same sources.

THE SOCIAL IDENTITY OF THE DOPE FIEND

One of my first surprises in talking with New York addicts was
the recurrent use by many of the term *dope fiend* to describe themselves and other addicts. Over and over I heard addicts use this disparaging term: "You know about dope fiends?" "He's a righteous
dope fiend." "I've been a dope fiend. . . ." "That's just like a dope
fiend."

My surprise at the use of "dope fiend" was not by any means
purely at the use of the term itself, because it is not a new term.
In fact, it is rather old-fashioned. During the 1920s and 1930s all
addicts were generally referred to as "dope fiends" by the public at
large. At the time addicts resented the term, and Alfred Lindesmith,
in his first book about addiction, *Opiate Addiction,* took great care
to demolish what he considered to be the public myth of the "dope
fiend." Lindesmith was successful in dismantling the myth, as both
professionals and the lay public gave up the use of the term. It

would seem that upon this abandonment the addicts took it up and in their usual inventive way with language gave it a novel use.

The term is used in two rather distinct ways. In one sense it is a parody of square society's image of and attitude toward drugs and drug users. In this parody all drugs—marijuana, pills, cough medicines, heroin, cocaine—become dope and all users are fiends. In its second sense it is more disparaging and more precise. With a slight inflection by the speaker it becomes a description of those addicts who have become completely identified with other addicts to the exclusion of anyone else. It describes someone whose whole life and nearly every moment is taken over by drugs or drug seeking, who has lost control of himself and his drug use, who is used by drugs rather than a drug user. It is, in short, a social identity among addicts.

Not all addicts by any means consider themselves dope fiends in this second sense. Urban addicts with short histories of heroin use, users who somehow manage to control their habits (keep them within some manageable parameters), users who avoid close association with addicts and who maintain relatively sustained relationships with the nonaddict society either through work, family, or friends, do not usually consider themselves to be "dope fiends." This was the case with one 30-year-old, black factory worker, who described himself this way:

> I always had a certain honor among addicts. I was never a dope fiend. I worked regular and didn't pull all that hustling and rip-off shit that most dope fiends do.

Neither medical addicts (those who became addicted during the process of some medical treatment) nor physician addicts consider themselves dope fiends.

Who then are the dope fiends? They are for the most part urban addicts who are overwhelmed by their addiction and must hustle on a sustained and continual basis to support their drug needs. The combination of uncontrolled drug use and regular hustling—in juxtaposition with the larger culture's mores, laws, and values about drug use—causes the development of a social identity distinct from addiction, which in a larger social context is seen as the addict subculture. Those addicts who somehow do not identify with the subculture are *not,* according to addicts, dope fiends; those who do, *are* dope fiends.

For the dope fiend heroin use is not necessarily a means to a particular end, but an end in itself. In the words of William Burroughs, ". . . the junk equation, junk is not like alcohol or weed, a means to increased enjoyment of life. Junk is not a kick. It is a way of life." [6] Heroin gives the dope fiend's life a purpose, a reason to be.

Life and the needs of most persons are complex and often perplexing. Needs and problems abound and sometimes overwhelm us; we find ourself in dilemmas about several competing needs. For the dope fiend life is much simpler. His need is clear and precise; he must have drugs over and above everything else. There is no battle of competing needs, but a single one that must be met every day. As a consequence of his uncontrolled habit, nearly all action is channeled toward the getting and the use of drugs.

Aside from heroin the dope fiend cares for little. Drugs and the activities necessary to get them become a focus for life, giving it a specific shape and purpose. Many dope fiends would not know what to do with themselves if they did not have to seek drugs every day. Alexander Trocchi, the English addict-novelist, expresses this well in his description of an American fellow addict:

> Without the stuff Tom's face takes on a strained expression; as the effect of the last fix wears off all grace dies within him. He becomes a dead thing. For him, ordinary consciousness is like a slow desert at the center of his being; his emphasis is suffocating. He tries to drink, to think of women, to remain interested, but his expression becomes shifty. The one vital cord in him is the bitter knowledge that he can choose to fix again. I have watched him. At the beginning he's over-confident. He laughs too much. But soon he falls silent and hovers restlessly at the edge of the conversation, as though he were waiting for the void of the drugless present to be miraculously filled (What would you do all day if you didn't have to look for a fix?). He is like a child dying of boredom, waiting for promised relief, until his expression becomes sullen. Then, when his face takes on a disdainful expression, I know he has decided to go and look for a fix.[7]

The dope fiend is turned inward to himself by his consuming need for drugs, and he expresses little concern for other activities, other people, and society. Family, friends, material objects, and achievement matter little to him. In many respects drugs and drug seeking become substitutes for relationships, material objects, and achievement. Dope fiends have other dope fiends, they have dope, and they have the satisfaction of getting the fix they need. What more do they need?

Other people matter little to the dope fiend; squares are particularly despised. Since society has forced him to hustle to satisfy

6. William Burroughs, *Junkie* (New York: Ace Books, Inc., 1953).
7. Alexander Trocchi, *Cain's Book* (New York: Grove Press, Inc., 1960), p. 78.

his need he comes to exploit nearly every situation and person he meets. With few exceptions the dope fiend uses other people for immediate personal gain; they become objects to be manipulated in any way possible to get what he needs. Dope fiends are ready to exploit any and all situations for possible gain, as was illustrated by a particularly winning Puerto Rican man who told me:

> You wouldn't believe the way I was when I was hustling. I'd go to visit an old friend (that I hadn't seen in years) an' I would pick out all the things I could steal and sell quick. Well, there's a color TV, a fan, an air-conditioner, a radio, a mixer. I always had my eyes open. Every house I went into I made an inventory for when I might have to come back.
>
> Why once'd I even called up an old girlfriend, arranged to meet her in a bar, an' went around to her apartment and cleaned her out when I knew she was out.

The exploitation of other persons and relationships must have a profound effect upon the dope fiend. One cannot have failed with wives, girlfriends, family, and friends and survive unscathed. How deep is the reservoir of guilt and remorse, how wide is the breadth of alienation that users must experience when so much of their action has been to exploit and deceive others? Some of this is hinted, if not specified, in the dope fiend's world view.

There is no future past the next fix for dope fiends. They are quite willing to drift from fix to fix, from day to day, with no concern for next week or next month, to say nothing of next year.

As a nation we Americans are an optimistic, hopeful people. The vast resources of the United States and the opportunities they give us to create a certain material comfort do not figure in the dope fiend's world. They do not attempt to attain material comfort or to seek a "better life" in the future. They are content "to be" and disdain the striving of straight society to achieve some future goal either as consummate achievers or equally prodigious consumers. Again Trocchi tells us, "One is no longer grotesquely involved in becoming, one simply is." [8]

In this respect dope fiends see themselves as having special knowledge about life, about the workings of society and its goals. They are the hip; straight society is square and chains itself to drab, dull, uninteresting existence. The life of the addict is seen by the dope fiend as exciting and meaningful in comparison to the monotonous workaday, 9-to-5, Saturday-night-at-the-bar existence of the straights. He sees himself as being more honest about himself and

8. Trocchi, *Cain's Book*, p. 19.

his existence than those who have cast him out. And maybe he is honest about his desire and pursuit of drugs; maybe his existence is more immediate than the vaguely outlined futuristic goals of his tormentors.

Oh yes, a dope fiend often talks of kicking, giving up drugs and living a square life. But this only occurs in moments of desperation when his habit has caught up with him, when he is without money, when he has developed a considerable tolerance and can't get high with his existing dosage, or when his defenses sag and society's stigmatization makes an inroad in his consciousness. The next moment he will fix and get off. It is only a small number of dope fiends who can maintain a constant disdain for society and its values and feel real comfort in their identity. Most are subject to waning and wavering periods of lost self-esteem. But who is so strong that he can live with the pariah status to which society has relegated to the addict?

Certainly the dope fiend's attitudes are a defense and a rationalization, but what is he to do if he is despised by society? He rises to the situation and affirms himself in the face of the antagonism. It is understandable human behavior and often ennobling to defend oneself against adversity. When, in the case of the addict, the adversary is society, the addict's acquiescence is not necessarily required or justified. It is *not* known that the dope fiend is indisputably wrong in his heroin use. Present society merely disdains its use and sees it as a threat. Indeed, the basis for society's response to opiate use may be its threat to the value of achievement.

Opiate use has not always been seen as a social problem. India in the 19th century had large numbers (estimated to be millions) of persons who used opiates in traditional and medicinal ways (usually drinking them in preparations or taking them in pill form) and never considered it a problem for which controls had to be established. On the other hand, China had millions of addicts at roughly the same time and considered it a grave social problem, to the point of fighting the powerful British in the Opium Wars. Richard Blum, in his "History of Opium," summarized the two divergent responses to opium use:

> At no time has India been described as having an opium problem in the sense that China did, in spite of the fact that India has been and is an opium-producing country and one in which access to and use of the drug have been widespread. . . . A considerable mystery remains as to why the Chinese instead of the Indians came either to decide abuse was present and/or suffer adverse effects. . . .[9]

9. Richard Blum, Drugs I: *Society and Drugs* (San Francisco: Jossey-Bass, Inc., 1969), p. 47.

THE SOCIETY OF DOPE FIENDS

As with other outcast or persecuted groups, both criminal and noncriminal, dope fiends band together in a defense of their position. This is the subculture of addiction called by Janet Clark the fantastic lodge:

> After the first six, eight months that I was making it, I never said, "Well, I'm a junkie." As an excuse or as anything. But now I say it constantly. I always refer to myself as a junkie, even when I'm not hooked or anything. And when you're introduced to somebody for the first time the first thing you find out is whether he's a junkie or not. It's like belonging to some fantastic lodge, you know, but the initiation ceremony is a lot rougher.[10]

Dope fiends claim that they can spot another dope fiend with only the most superficial contact, in many instances without having talked to the other person. Both physical addiction and the attitudes of the dope fiend are said to be apparent in gestures and stance—"in the way he holds himself." In some respects this ability to identify each other, which is as good an indicator as one can find of the existence of a dope-fiend subculture, serves as a means of protection against undercover police. But this is only one of several functions that the dope-fiend subculture serves.

Its principal function is to provide the addict an opportunity to meet others like himself and in the coming together benefit from whatever association or comradeship develops. This obviously enhances his morale and gives him some defense against the antagonistic larger society. Many dope fiends claim they cannot get along with straight people, that they cannot talk with them and have little in common. Most of us gravitate toward persons like ourselves —persons who share age, attitudes, interests, or occupations—because we find them easy to communicate with. Dope fiends find similar comfort among other dope fiends.

These associations also put the addict directly into the drug market, both as a consumer and as a seller. An addict with only a single source of drugs operates under a decided disadvantage. If a connection is busted or is otherwise unavailable he is left without a ready source of a drug that he may need several times a day. Close association with other addicts increases his chance of finding several

10. Helen MacGill Hughes (ed.), *The Fantastic Lodge* (Greenwich, Conn.: Fawcett World Library, Premier Books, 1971).

drug sources. It is advantageous for an addict to immerse himself in the addict subculture; the more addicts he knows, the greater opportunity he has to cop drugs. Long association with dope fiends puts him in direct contact with drug sellers, at one or several levels. This naturally enhances his functioning as a consumer and opens opportunities to sell drugs as well.

Drug sellers have to be extremely cautious to avoid detection and arrest. Their best protection is to avoid completely selling anything to strangers, who are often undercover police, and to sell only to users who are known and can be trusted not to be informers. Relationships in the dope-fiend culture allow the seller to know those who buy from him and, therefore, help protect him against arrest. At the same time information is circulated about addict informers or potential informers.

On the negative side the dope-fiend culture reinforces the addict's alienation from society, defines him as a criminal to the larger "respectable" society, and impedes his ability to overcome his addiction. In general the existing laws, the repressive drug policies, and attitudes in our society drive the addict underground. These factors —in combination with the dope-fiend culture—tend to cut him off from nonaddict associations and, fulfilling the prophecy, cause him to become a repeating offender.

This is most apparent when dope fiends attempt to give up drugs. Even when the effort is genuine and is not made to pacify the demands of some immediate societal pressure the addict, because of his alienation, may be forced back into drugs simply because he knows no one else but addicts. Life is hard and lonely without friends and associates. If special efforts are not made to make nonaddict friends and to avoid dope fiends the addict's efforts to give up heroin are perilous and shaky. Relationships and attitudes that aided him as an addict can sabotage his efforts to change his life. It would seem that the dope fiend's cynical dictum, "once an addict, always an addict," can—with the sheer power of the drug—lock the dope fiend into a seemingly perpetual system.

IN JAIL AND IN TREATMENT

The addict in jail and under treatment seems to be a different person than he is on the street. Maverick and nonconforming on the street, in institutions he adapts easily and readily learns to "do his time" or "become rehabilitated." This may be a general acquiescence to authority and its force or it may be a credit to the addict's adaptability—to his general ability to ride with "changes" and to survive unpleasant situations and pressures.

In situations where the full pressure of society and its laws and mores are brought to bear against him the addict accommodates readily to institutions and institution games. In jail and prison he learns easily how to do his prison time, how to avoid unnecessary violence and get out as quickly as possible. In treatment he learns to play the treatment games and easily becomes "rehabilitated." In short, he learns how to give the right answers to his keepers and treaters.

Inside an institution he is often very optimistic about his ability to resist heroin and give up drug use; he appears eager to return to the fold of square society. He is usually ready and able to tell his treaters or keepers that dope is not worth the hazards of incarceration or coercive treatment and that he is going to give it up. Occasionally an angry young beginning addict or an experienced old dope fiend will frankly say that he does not *wish* or is *not able* to give up heroin use, but on the whole most will present a convincing act of rehabilitation and a story of good intentions upon release. This is not by any means all fiction or self-delusion; many do not realize the full power of heroin and the strength of their addiction and genuinely believe that they can give up drugs whenever they decide to.

That most addicts relapse and eventually become readdicted to heroin after leaving treatment or release from prison is a chilling fact. Indeed, the recurrence of these relapses is one of the factors that makes narcotic addiction the social problem that it is. A small number of addicts experience a sort of natural remission (the percentages are generally unknown but it is thought to be approximately 5%), and still others give up heroin for alcohol, which while legal is probably more destructive of their health and lives than heroin ever was.

Prison offers little to the addict except the association of other addicts. Quite often incarceration causes the beginning addict to become more entrenched in dope-fiend society. It often gives him more contacts and more information—as illustrated by this quote from an interview with a 19-year-old black addict:

> Before I ever went to the joint I didn't know anything about dope or copping. Oh, I used it, but I really didn't know much about it. The first time I went to Riker's Island I got a good education. I learned all about dope—where to get the best, how to cut it, differ-

ent ways to use it. When I got out I could cop in any one of the five boroughs. I met dope fiends from all over New York; I wasn't confined to Bedford Stuyvesant (Brooklyn) anymore. And when I hit the streets I started dealing dope for the first time.

Imprisonment also bestows upon the addict the identity of convict. Essentially the convict code is one of a personal laissez faire. John Irwin describes this very well in his 1970 book *The Felon*:

> Committment to the convict code or the identity of the convict is to a high degree a lifetime committment to do your own time; that is, to live and let live, and when you feel that someone is not letting you live, to either take it, leave, or stop him yourself, but never call for help from *official agencies of control*. [my emphasis]

This attitude or set of attitudes generally reinforces the other identities of the hustler-dope fiend and serves to set him still further apart from the larger society. The larger society requires a personal attitude different from that fostered by convict life. One is expected to do more than "live and let live"; one is expected to comment and act upon others' behavior; one is expected *not* to take the law into one's own hands but to go to the police or the courts when other persons violate one's rights or person. But this is not the way of convicts or hustler-addicts, and any individual who attempted to live by square standards in an addict's world would be at a decided disadvantage and would have to adapt.

"Rehabilitation" is only a little different from incarceration and is in most cases only a halfway measure. The addict may get help with his personal or family problems, learn how to barber or lay floor tiles, and get his high-school diploma through a general education test in a treatment and rehabilitation program, but never really change his attitude toward drug use or learn how to manage life in his old neighborhood with its myriad pitfalls and temptations, how to make square friends, and how to live without heroin. Except in the case of well-run self-help residential programs and methadone maintenance clinics that have strong social-service components, treatment offers the addict little. More often than not he goes to treatment to avoid some pressure being exerted upon him; seldom is it because he wants to give up drugs. If an abstention program is not aware of the addict's motivations and actually tests them, the program comes to be used by the addict in ways that were never intended: as a service, rather than as rehabilitation; as a temporary shelter; as a place in which to clean up in order to get high again or to manage one's habit more easily. Compulsory programs like the civil committment programs of California and New York and the U.S. Public Hospitals at Lexington, Kentucky, and Ft. Worth, Texas, are almost universally either ineffective or effective only with nonaddicts who were somehow apprehended while experimenting with opiates.

If the addict himself comes to feel that his drug use and the life associated with it is dysfunctional, that life is really too difficult as an addict, then he will make some genuine effort to abstain on his own or enter treatment. Voluntary abstention is more common than writing on addiction would suggest. A substantial number of addicts do give up heroin use for long or short periods of time outside of institutions, but relapse is nearly always a continual threat. During such periods of voluntary abstention the addict manages to make a reasonable social adjustment and lead a reasonably productive life. Most work, get along with their families, and tend to avoid heavy hustling; when they substitute a drug it is usually a legal one —alcohol.

There are, of course, many involuntary abstentions forced upon the addict, those that result from imprisonment or stays in compulsory treatment programs. So much of the addict's time in prison and treatment is taken up by drug talk and drug fantasies, that it would seem that he is only cleaning up, waiting for the day he can get out to use heroin and get high again. Conversation among addicts in such places continually hinges on drugs. Stories are told and retold about the best drugs, best highs, biggest sales. These seem to act as a primer on the pump to prepare the addict to use heroin upon release, to assure him an easy return to the old life.

THE EX-ADDICT IDENTITY

Most abstaining ex-addicts and persons maintained in methadone clinics are "cool" about their earlier life as heroin users. Most are content to put that life behind them, to put it out of sight, to emphasize their present rather than their past life. However, with the growth of self-help and religious treatment programs, there have been a growing number of highly visible ex-addicts, a growing number who assume active ex-addict identities. These are persons who actively talk about their earlier addiction, who proselytize for various drug programs, and who attempt to prevent the spread of drug abuse by offering personal testimony.

The active ex-addict seems to have made an asset out of a past life that was denigrated and despised by society. The experience as an addict is used, and occasionally exploited, as a valid qualification for work in various drug programs. This parallels the general trend in the United States toward putting formal educational qualifications in a more realistic perspective and giving recognition and credit for the individual's experience; there has been a proliferation of paraprofessionals in many of the service and helping professions associated with drug treatment, education, and prevention programs. There is, in addition, a sympathy bestowed upon the ex-addict that is not unlike that given to the reclaimed sinner who has changed his ways and come back to the fold of society. Add to this an element of the glamor that attaches itself to men (not women) who have countered society's morals and laws, and one finds a certain mystique bestowed upon the ex-addict.

In keeping with the repentant-sinner approach of many fundamental Christian groups, drug programs, nonreligious as well as religious, often use the testimony of ex-addicts in drug-education and prevention programs. The ex-addicts go before local community groups to make personal confessions of the evils of drug use and its associated life. With graphic stories of their own experiences, they instruct the naive and young to be careful with drugs and to avoid the pitfalls of their own drug experiences. The audiences are usually responsive and appreciative of these techniques and express the opinion that the ex-addict's experience, which is "where it is really at," is more dramatic and valid than drastic lectures by persons who have never used drugs themselves. They are probably correct in their attitudes.

Drug programs use this ex-addict approach in two ways: to reach and solicit the support of local communities, and to counter the approach of the more traditionally operated, professionally dominated programs. Individuals sometimes use the experience for their own personal gain. One especially articulate and colorful ex-addict, upon leaving Synanon, made extensive testimonial tours up and down the East Coast of the United States, both to earn money and to solicit job offers. But most are less mercenary and play the professional ex-addict role out of some mixture of personal gain, a personal zeal to prevent drug abuse, and satisfaction in communicating their ideas and ideology to a wide audience.

That the ex-addict's world view is quite different from the dope fiend's is not startling. Both the active, self-conscious proselytizer and the "cooler" ex-addict assume a different attitude toward the future, become more concerned about human relationships, and demonstrate an appreciation for material objects. And so ex-addicts plan marriage and family life, make square friends, open bank accounts, and buy large ostentatious cars in keeping with the values of the larger American society.

This is more dramatic and sudden for the active ex-addict than for the cooler less visible one, but that is because society's confirmation of recognition and status is more obvious and deliberate in drug treatment programs than it is in the local community. The active ex-addict gets considerably more feedback from his local community and from larger society as the drug program gives him an obvious place and a productive role to play vis-à-vis both.

Fortunately, the conversion to square society is not always as complete or as encompassing as the ex-addict, drug programs, and society would have one believe, for the ex-addict often remains something of a hustler, "cool cat," or "dude." The difference between the behavior of the addict and of the ex-addict hustler is that society condones the ex-addict's hustles—his ability to raise money and materials, to gain local community support, and so forth—and that he operates more-or-less within the laws and mores of society. In effect, he joins the society of "smooth businessmen," "shrewd bankers," and "academic grantsmen." He joins the society of those who build "successful careers," who "get things done." He joins the bulk of American society "on the make."

THE ROAD TRAVELED

Outlining the major stages of the career of an addict as I have makes it appear to be the road traveled by each and every addict. This is far from true, for as there are different addicts (young and old, male and female, rich and poor), there are different roads through the career process. Not by any means does every addict become a hustler, a dope fiend, a convict, and a rehabilitant or ex-addict, in that order. Some short cut the process and never go to jail or treatment, never steal to support their habits, never become dope fiends. One very successful administrator of a large program in New York City used heroin for only eight months and stole only casually to support his habit and never went to jail before becoming a zealous, vociferous, convincing ex-addict.

Some addicts manage to maintain their ties with their families, keep their jobs, and sustain a certain honor in dealing with others that keeps them from assuming completely the dope fiend identity. Some people can live in both worlds; they can use dope and still keep their jobs and their square, nondrug-using friends. Others never stop being dope fiends; for them dope is an end in itself, the apex of their lives. Still others die following a precarious and hazardous career. And then there are those who only come out at the far side to become helpless victims of alcoholism—itself another career.

Only a small number of addicts in the United States become ex-addicts. As a nation we have given them little help. There has been very little serious treatment (and that only recently); there has been, instead, a heavy, moralistic attitude that has dictated incarceration and coercion. If anything, we have made it nearly impossible for the addict to survive the enforced imprisonment and coercive treatment programs we have erected to deal with the problem of addiction.

An addict has had to be strong and willful to sustain himself through all the incarceration, all the "rehabilitation," all the stigma that society has thrust upon him. Despite our fears and the repulsion we feel for heroin and heroin users, there is no real moral justification for society's condoning the ways the police and the courts treat the addict, the way society has made him a scapegoat for all of its ills, and the abysmal life we have forced upon him. Our official attitude toward the addict is unequivocally irrational and unnecessary. It is simply another manifestation—like our gross materialism, like our penchant for illogical wars, like our irrational foreign policies—of our particular national madness.

[2]

Becoming a Heroin Addict

One of the few achievements, perhaps the only one, of the propaganda efforts (one can hardly call them educational or preventive efforts) of the old Federal Bureau of Narcotics was the development of the stereotype of the drug seller and the ways in which he initiated persons into drug use and abuse. This stereotype characterized the seller as a depraved profiteer who would do anything to create new users, thus assuring a ready and eager market for his sales. The motives of the seller were pure malice and profit as he skulkingly waited for innocent and unsuspecting persons (usually children) to offer them drugs, addiction, and "eventual enslavement." In this description, all the naive victim need do was use the offered drug and he would be on a sure road to addiction.

To anyone who knew anything about drug users or addiction this stereotype was obviously erroneous. Drug sellers do not have to tempt or entice persons to use drugs; drug users usually seek out the seller. A single use of any opiate—even of the most powerful, heroin—will not cause a person to become addicted. But this simple-minded view of the drug seller and beginning drug use lived a long time, much too long a time. As recently as 1962 the White House Conference on Drug Abuse heard serious testimony from law-enforcement officials that propounded this view. To this day the hard line taken by police, city officials, and state legislators against drug sellers, founded upon the belief that users and sellers are different persons, reflects this stereotype.

The reasons that this stereotype has lived so long have to do with the power of the Federal Bureau of Narcotics and the failure of scientists to specify and test the more plausible and now current theory of initial drug use, i.e., that initial use of heroin occurs in a cultural and social setting that encourages and facilitates its use.

The Federal Bureau of Narcotics had, until the late 1950s, *nearly* complete domination over all other sources of information and research about illicit drug use and addiction. A good deal of the information about narcotic addiction going to legislators and the public was unfounded scientifically and filtered through a narrow enforcement perspective. This domination was so complete they could and did arrest doctors who dared to treat addicts privately and intimidate scientists who disagreed with them or propounded other views and theories. For years Dr. Lawrence Kolb and sociologist Alfred Lindesmith were the only persons strong enough and brave enough to stand up to their blatant propaganda. With the 1950s the power of the Bureau declined, and by the time Bureau Chief Harry T. Anslinger retired in 1962 it had taken a back seat to scientists and people actively treating addicts as sources of information on narcotic addiction and associated activities of addicts.

Researchers and writers in the field failed because they were too often seeking single or all-inclusive causes for narcotic addiction instead of just looking at the simple processes of initial use and addiction. Everyone was too busy with the grand theory to deal with simple processes. As a consequence, there were a number of elaborate theories, which anyone and everyone disputed, and few data to substantiate them. The research literature is replete with small samples, 10, 20, and 30 addicts, from which generalization is difficult; so even the best theories went begging for empirical support.

INITIAL USE

Information and data about initial use of heroin, or of other drugs for that matter, are still very sketchy. Few researchers have systematically investigated initial heroin use, as distinct from heroin addiction. To date there have been only two empirical studies that deal with initial heroin use; both of these were primarily concerned with the causes of addiction and gave only passing attention to the processes of addiction (beginning use, habituation, physical addiction, detoxification, abstention, relapse, and so forth). Bingham Dai, in his original, classic study of 40 addicts in Chicago, found that most of his small sample acquired their information about the effects of opiates through association with other opiate users and felt certain social pressures to use the drug.[1] In a 1951 study of 22 adolescent, male, heroin addicts at Bellevue Hospital in New York it was found that they were commonly introduced to heroin either by a heroin seller or by another boy who was addicted.[2]

Our data support the idea that initial heroin use is a social phenomenon; the role of other persons in the initial use of heroin is crucial. Beginning heroin use is *not* a solitary activity. Persons are initiated in a group situation among friends and acquaintances. Only 17 (4%) of our sample of 417 males reported that they were alone the first time they used heroin; by far the majority (96%) reported that they used heroin the first time with one or more persons. These other persons were almost always friends and were usually of the same sex. White persons in our sample tended to use in larger groups than did blacks and Puerto Ricans.

More often than not the persons who initiated the men and boys of our sample into heroin use had used it previously themselves. Some were addicted, but most were not. Let me illustrate this with some quotes about the circumstances of first use:

> I was at a party with about ten of my friends—both guys and girls. Someone asked me whether I would like to try some horse. I was high on alcohol at the time, so I said I was game for it. That dude who turned me on was a user, not an addict.

> I was at a discotheque with these two motorcycle dudes; they hung out there. I was just starting to run with them and was with a group of four or five guys. . . . We had been drinking a little beer earlier and one of them suggested we get some H. We left the discotheque to cop. I got off in a car—mainlined. I vomited and got stoned. After a while we all went back to the discotheque and had a good time.

> The first time I used I snorted with two friends in one of their houses. One of them had tried H before and said it was a good high, so I tried it. We were going to a dance and I wanted to be high for the dance.

> The first time I used heroin . . . I wanted to be one of the fellows. I was with my girlfriend and a friend and we got rapping about dope.

1. Bingham Dai, *Opiate Addiction in Chicago* (Shanghai: The Commercial Press, 1937).

2. Paul Zimmering, James Toolan, Ranate Safrin, and Bernard S. Wortis, "Heroin Addiction in Adolescent Boys," in *The Journal of Nervous and Mental Disease,* 114 (1951).

My buddy said he knew where to get some (he had used before) and so I gave him some money. We got off, but I wouldn't let my girlfriend try it.

Only a minority reported that they were initiated by persons who sold heroin, and some said that they themselves were selling heroin before they actually used it:

I knew this pusher dude. You wouldn't believe the money he had; he had a green Eldorado and the best clothes you ever saw. Well, I was on my way to meet two friends one day (they were both using heroin) an' I see this dude standing on the corner an' he looked groovy. So I asked what it was made him look so good. He said it was smack an' I said I wanted some. He gave it to me.

I was dealing marijuana, hash, and heroin. I had been into "smoke" [marijuana] for a long time, but I never tried heroin. I guess I got curious. I had been dealing heroin for about four months and one day a friend asked me for some and got off (skin-popped) in front of me. Seeing him get off made me want to try it, so I did.

USE OF OTHER DRUGS BEFORE HEROIN

By the time they get to heroin, most persons have had experience with other drugs; heroin is seldom the first used. More than three out of four (77%) of the men we interviewed reported that they had used marijuana before heroin. Only small minorities had used barbiturates (13%), airplane glue (11%), amphetamines (6%), cocaine (6%), and LSD (5%) before. This high incidence of marijuana use does not mean, however, that everyone who uses marijuana (or any other drug for that matter) will become a heroin user; that is another story. Such an argument is like saying that everyone who smokes tobacco will turn to marijuana. Certainly there is an association between tobacco use and marijuana use, but one does not either lead to or cause the other.[3]

I expect that most persons had also used alcohol by that time, but unfortunately the data collected on alcohol use are not available. Questions about it were asked in our follow-up questionnaire, which, however, has never been analyzed because the funds for the completion of the project were curtailed.

In general, the middle-class pattern of wide experimentation

3. Two recent books have dealt with the relationship between marijuana and heroin use: John Kaplan, *Marijuana: The New Prohibition*, (New York: World Publishing Company, 1970) and Michael Schofield, *The Strange Case of Pot* (Harmondsworth, England: Penguin Books, 1971).

with a variety of drugs, progressing from marijuana to LSD, barbiturates, and amphetamines and then to heroin, does not apply to the majority of New York addicts. This may be the result of the accessibility of drugs on the illegal markets and the greater availability of heroin, but it may also involve differing attitudes and beliefs about the effects of drugs. Many of those with whom I spoke paid no lip service to "Timothy Leary ideologies" and were not the least bit concerned with "consciousness expanding" drugs such as LSD and mescaline, saying that kind of high was not for them and that LSD was "another trip," implying that it was one trip that they were not interested in taking. Curiously, only a few persons connected any "consciousness expansion" rationals with marijuana.

There were, however, exceptions to this general rule. Young, short term users of heroin; those under 20 years old who had used heroin for four years or less; and white users, who were more often middle-class, tended to fit the pattern of wide experimentation before heroin use more than older users and blacks did.[4]

WHY HEROIN?

A number of reasons are given for beginning the use of heroin. Some users cited emotional states involving problems with families or girlfriends, but the majority fell into two categories: 38% said that they were curious about the effects of heroin and wanted to experience it themselves, and 36% said that their friends were using it and they wanted to try it also.

Obviously, persons may use heroin for a combination of reasons—psychological, social, and intellectual. One 19-year-old boy from the Bronx cited all three in his description of his first use:

> I was feeling down. I had got down [had sexual intercourse] with my older brother and was packing a lot of guilt. I didn't want my friends to know what happened. A couple of days later I was in a basement with a buddy. He had used and was strung out. He offered me some and I was curious to know what it was like. I skin-popped, got high (felt real comfortable) and then drowsy. I guess I was trying to prove myself to my friend; I wanted to show him and the others that I could do what they were doing.

Motives for human behavior are often complex, as the above quote suggests. At any given time it may be difficult for an individ-

4. For a more detailed report of this data see John Langrod, "Secondary Drug Use Among Heroin Users," in *The International Journal of the Addictions*, Vol. 5, no. 4 (1970).

ual to account for all or even a few of the reasons for the things he does. Often we do not know why we do things; the motives remain subconscious. Without an in-depth study of the complex motivations for beginning heroin use—no such study has been made although there has been a lot of speculation—I believe we can safely accept what addicts have told us about the pressures of a friend's use and the intellectual motive of curiosity. Experience of other drugs, marijuana and alcohol in most cases, and some association with drug users or addicts could invoke such curiosity. Users and addicts talk among themselves and with others a great deal about the effects of heroin, comparing euphorias, qualities, and so forth. One would not have to be unduly curious to decide to experience the drug personally—particularly in the current cultural climate of drug exploration. I myself am curious to know what the effects of heroin are, particularly because addicts seem so willing to give up so much to use it. The point I wish to make is that initial use of heroin is not as clouded in complex motivations as many persons would have us believe. It is, perhaps, not unlike the beginning use of other legal and illegal drugs—alcohol, tobacco, and marijuana—all of which occur in settings in which there are certain pressures toward use.

Unlike the small-town, Southern addict described by John O'Donnell [5] and the physician addicts studied by Charles Winick, [6] only one of the men of our sample attributed his initial use of heroin to the need for relief of physical pain. This was an ingenuous Puerto Rican I met at Manhattan State Hospital.

> I was working at a paint factory at the time; it was heavy, kinda back-breaking work. One Sunday I was playing ball up in Central Park, you know I always keep busy with sports, and hurt my back sliding into third base. I was really in pain when I went to work on Monday. I could hardly stoop over. After about an hour on the job I told the guys I was working with that I was going to have to go home. Well, one of them said, "Try some of this," pulling a cap of white powder out of his pocket. I snorted it, just a little, and felt wonderful. I couldn't believe how good I felt; I worked like a whirl-wind all the rest of the day.
>
> Well, the next day he sold me some more and I used it every day for two weeks. Then I started to get sick, and that's when I found out what I had been using.

Most persons felt positive effects from heroin the first time they used it. Nearly two-thirds (63%) of the men in our sample

5. John A. O'Donnell, *Narcotic Addicts in Kentucky* (Washington: U.S. Government Printing Office, 1970).

6. Charles Winick, "Physician Addicts," in *Social Problems*, Fall (1963).

reported that they felt positive effects upon first use, while another 27% said they felt positive effects from the second to the fifth time. Rather surprisingly, seven men (2%) reported that they had *never* experienced positive effects from heroin use.

More white persons in our sample reported positive effects on first use (71%) than blacks (64%) and Puerto Ricans (57%). This may be explained by the white men's wider exploration of other drugs before the initial use of heroin; having experienced more drugs they may be more susceptible to the euphoric effects of heroin.

The most common first-use response was nausea and vomiting, followed by a euphoria that the respondents described as being different from and more intense than that produced by other drugs. This was described by one 19-year-old in a way that leads one to think that the effect for him was one of self-actualization, an effect that gave him new vitality:

> My brother was using at the time; he later became addicted too. The two of us were pretty close, closer than anyone else, and I thought a lot of him. I wanted to see what made my brother take it. Well, I found out. When I got off the first time, I felt like me. I felt alive. Before I used heroin I was always down; I didn't have any energy. When I was high I was something else.

Most described it as an unusually pleasant euphoria that permitted a different perspective on themselves and their world. For example, this description was given by a rather precise, but otherwise inarticulate, 20-year-old:

> It was nice. It brought you into a cloud [from which] you see the world better, with a good outlook. I was like out there remote from the world.

Some said that they did not feel any positive effects with the first use, only nausea, vomiting, and headaches. In subsequent use they did experience the euphoria, however, which suggests that, as with marijuana, some persons have to learn how to respond to the drug, how to make themselves more susceptible to its effects.

EVENTUAL ADDICTION

Subsequent use and eventual addiction for the men in our sample was a slow, rather gradual process. This was discovered by calculating the mean time between the different methods of use and also the time between initial use and discovery of physical dependence. The initial method of use for the majority was "snorting," sniffing the drug through the nose. Only a very few "mainlined," injected the drug directly into a vein, the first time they used. The majority continued to snort for a while; then, either because their nasal membranes became inflamed or because they learned and desired more immediate effects, they soon began "skin-popping," injecting the drug subcutaneously. Eventually the users discovered that the euphoric effects came much faster with direct injection into a vein.

We found that the mean time between their initial use of heroin and the first time they mainlined was four months.[7] The majority (66%) complete the process in less than 6 months, with the more precocious getting down to the serious business of mainlining in less than a month.

As in beginning use, subsequent use during the first year usually takes place with other persons. Three out of every four (75%) said that they usually used heroin with others during their first year of use, while only one in ten (11%) reported that they usually used alone during that period.

There are a number of purely mechanical reasons for this association with other heroin users. The beginning user usually does not have a ready source of supply (a "connection") and must rely upon others to buy the drug for him. Usually the beginner will seek out a friend who has a source who then cops for both of them. Similarly the neophyte may not possess the "works" for injecting the drug and must rely upon others for that also. Actual injection is also something that must be learned from others; it requires considerable skill and some practice to inject oneself with the often dull needles that many use. Actually, works, although rather crudely made, are far easier to use than the standard syringe.

Although our project did not explore the specific reasons for continued use after the first use, I believe that the reason for most persons was quite simple: they enjoyed the first experiences and continued the practice. For those for whom it took longer to get a positive effect, other motives, psychological or social, may have come into play until such a time as a positive effect was experienced. This was illustrated by a close friend of mine who, during a year of intensive drug use, used heroin three times:

7. By far the majority of our sample mainlined—96% in fact; 87% reported that it was the usual method of use, while another 9% said that they mainlined occasionally.

I used smeeck three times. I kept bugging my cousin to try some. He was a pretty heavy shooter who managed to control it and didn't get addicted. The first time I just got sick and felt drowsy. The second time was about the same as the first. I found out what it was all about the third time; it was fantastic. I knew after that that I could never take it again; I liked it too much. I knew I wasn't getting the effect the first two times. Bernie told me I wasn't getting it. I wanted to feel what he felt.

Heroin users and addicts are right, in some respects, when they say that one should not knock heroin until one has experienced it; often the drug allows the user to manage anxieties and feelings and lets him function better. This is in addition to the usual euphoria. Admittedly these "good effects" are induced artificially and one can assume that they will only last as long as the drug is effective, but for some it assuages deep and real anxieties and tensions. It gives them something akin to artist Roy Litchenstein's vision of "Peace Through Chemistry," a mechanical peace.

Let me illustrate some of these "good effects" with a cross-section of answers we got to the question, "What did heroin do for you?" asked informally of a small group of residents of Hart Island:

It gave me peace of mind. I could get away from reality and forget my complexes. Straight, I felt I couldn't relate to people, and when I used drugs [heroin] I could communicate better.

I liked getting high. It was a good feeling. Heroin made me feel secure. I really felt protected. When I was high nothing could hurt me.

Heroin makes you forget about your problems; makes you feel you know everything. You feel strong and healthy, not weak. You can work.

These responses were from persons in an active antidrug environment who could not deny that heroin gave them something they enjoyed. When it offers some so much, it is no wonder that the use of the drug has, for centuries, been so hard to control.

Many persons knew before they used heroin what addiction entailed and had observed what happened to addicts and how they were treated by society. Indeed, many of the persons I interviewed during the study said that while growing up they had detested addicts and had believed that addiction was something that would never happen to them. This realization did not deter them, however, as most believed that they could control their use of heroin and not become addicted.

Not all who use heroin or opiates become addicted. Lee Robins, in an important study made in 1967 of a population of "normal," black men attending an elementary school in St. Louis, Missouri, in 1932, found that 13% of 221 men had tried heroin at some time in their lives and that four out of five of these (10% of the total sample) became addicted.[8] Some try heroin and like the effects but do not wish to risk the possible addiction. I know two such persons: one whom I mentioned earlier, and another who used opium ten times while he served in the Peace Corps in Asia. He used it out of curiosity and had no intention of using it again, although he enjoyed it. I suppose it remains to be seen if they will or will not become addicted, but I doubt that either will.

Unfortunately, none of the people in our sample were so able to control their use; all were either addicted or considered in danger of becoming addicted. However, addiction is a slower process than one would think. The average time between first use and the realization of physical addiction was 11 months. This time could be as short as three weeks and as long as six years, for that was the range of time between the two events. One could say that some persons are particularly susceptible to heroin. One man told me that after he first used heroin he used it every day for six years until the time he was committed by his family to treatment. He claimed that he was addicted the first time that he used it but did not experience physical withdrawal until the fourth week of use.

PATTERNS OF CONTINUING AND SECONDARY DRUG USE

As we saw earlier, the middle-class pattern of drug use that begins with marijuana and LSD and progresses to barbiturates and amphetamines and, eventually, heroin use does not apply to our urban working-class addicts. The New York addict uses a wide variety of drugs other than heroin and alcohol, but most of his secondary drug use occurs after heroin use and addiction, not before.

An average of 3.4 drugs other than heroin and alcohol was used with any frequency (more than six times), with more than half (55%) of the sample reporting having used four or more other drugs and more than a quarter (28%), six or more other drugs. Length of heroin use and the ethnicity of the user seem to be closely associated with the number of drugs used. The longer men used heroin, the more secondary drugs they reported, which suggests that

8. Lee Robins, "Drug Use in a Normal Population of Young Negro Men," in *The American Journal of Public Health*, Vol. 57, no. 9 (1967).

long-term users may find themselves in situations where they are less selective about the drugs they use and take whatever they can get. That is to say, perhaps, that drugs tend to use them rather than the reverse. White addicts may also be "used by drugs," because they reported more drugs used than either blacks or Puerto Ricans. The mean number of secondary drugs reported by whites was 4.6, as compared to 3.2 for Puerto Ricans and 2.7 for blacks. But averages are only half the story; more than half (51%) of the whites reported using six or more other drugs, while only a quarter (25%) of the Puerto Ricans and less than one out of five (18%) of the blacks used that many.

After heroin, which everyone used, and marijuana, which nearly everyone used (92%), cocaine, barbiturates, amphetamines, and methadone were, in that order, the drugs cited most often. Two out of three (66%) of the sample said that they had used cocaine at least once, with nearly half (47%) reporting that they had used it more than six times. In the recent past, cocaine was considered by street addicts as something of a luxury because of its then high cost —$10 to $15 a cap—but recently the supply has increased considerably and the price has dropped in New York to $5 to $7, making it more available. Cocaine, as well as being taken separately, is often taken in combination with heroin; this is called "speedballing" and is said to intensify the "rush" of drugs effects. Blacks show a certain preference for "coke"; like heroin, it is readily available in Harlem and other black communities in New York, with more than half (54%) the blacks reporting that they had used it more than six times.

Barbiturates and amphetamines were usually used as substitutes for heroin or in conjunction with it, and only seldom exclusively. During periods when addicts cannot get heroin, whether because they do not have the money or have lost their connections or because of a local panic when heroin becomes scarce, they may simply substitute barbiturates until such a time as they can get heroin again. Both barbiturates and amphetamines may also be used to supplement heroin when the addict's tolerance for heroin has progressed past his ability to get the dosage needed to obviate withdrawal and keep him just normal, to say nothing of getting high.

Amphetamines, including methedrine, are used often in combination with heroin, but once a person has used heroin, they are seldom used singly. Many Puerto Ricans from the *Barrio,* or East Harlem, use ampules of injectable methedrine called "bombitas," or "little bombs," to "speed" them up to go out to hustle.

Unlike the white, Southern addict described by researchers at

Lexington Hospital [10] methadone in its pill form (known commer-
cially as dolophines and in the drug argot as "dollies") is rarely used
by New York addicts as a primary drug of addiction. New York
heroin users prefer the heightened euphoria of heroin or cocaine to
the blunted euphoria of methadone. Frequently dollies are used to
kick or cut down on the addict's habit without his having to go to
a hospital or a doctor; they permit him to control his heroin habit
and to continue to feel its effects without the massive doses that are
needed when tolerances are high. One-third (37%) of the sample
reported using dollies, with a quarter (26%) reporting using them
more than six times.

Usually white addicts were more likely than blacks and Puerto
Ricans to abuse secondary drugs other than heroin and to use drugs
such as LSD, barbiturates, and amphetamines before heroin. This
may be the result of the sheer availability of certain drugs. The
major heroin traffic in New York City is concentrated in black and
Puerto Rican neighborhoods (the black ghettoes of Central Harlem,
Bedford-Stuyvesant in Brooklyn, and the South Bronx, and their
Puerto Rican counterparts in East Harlem and Williamsburg). But
the abuse of secondary drugs by whites may also be an expression of
more severe psychological problems, as John Langrod suggests:

> Although whites are more likely than blacks and Puerto Ricans to
> come from intact homes, earn more money, graduate from high
> school, not have addicted or alcoholic relatives, or be on welfare;
> they are less likely to have gotten along with their families, prior to
> and during heroin addiction, and are less optimistic about getting
> along with their families upon leaving the institution. It is possible
> that whites, despite their favorable social circumstances, may be using
> drugs because of more severe emotional problems compared to blacks
> and Puerto Ricans, for which drug use may be more of a social phe-
> nomenon or an escape from a genuinely oppressive social-economic
> reality.[11]

HOW LONG IS A RUN?

It is my impression that heroin use by addicts is much more
periodic than most of the research and literature on the topic suggest. Actually there is as yet no real information about the extent or

10. Joseph Spira, John C. Ball, and Emily S. Cottrell, "Addictions to Methadone Among Patients at Lexington and Fort Worth," in *Public Health Reports*,
Vol. 83, no. 8 (1968).
11. John Langrod, "Secondary Drug Use," p. 633.

periodicity of heroin use by addicts, and our study did not deal with it either. In the absence of solid research on the topic, my impressions may offer some information on a subject that has not yet been treated in any systematic way.

I became interested in this after I observed that most addicts spend a good part of their careers in addiction in jail and that many make occasional but real efforts to abstain from heroin use after incarceration or treatment. An addict may say that he has been addicted for 13 years, but as you delve into his history you may learn that 6 years of that time have been spent in jail, another year in various treatment programs, and, perhaps, 6 months in actual abstention outside of an institution.[12] The actual duration of physical addiction and heroin use is often much shorter and more sporadic than one would expect from the original, superficial report. What many persons may be describing is not the length of actual physical addiction but the length of time they have considered themselves addicts—which for many may be more a social status than a physical condition.

This periodicity of drug use is illustrated in my field report of an interview with Beverly, an attractive 22-year-old white woman who was in Manhattan Rehabilitation Center:

> Beverly began the use of opiates (dilaudid) when she was 17 years old. She was initiated by an older boyfriend and used every day for 3 months after her first use (from supplies stolen from a drug store by the boyfriend). After an argument with the same boyfriend she kicked cold turkey and left the boyfriend and her home town to travel to Michigan with another boyfriend she had gone with earlier. At that time she was off drugs for one month.

> During the trip to Michigan she became pregnant; when she returned home she realized her condition. Shortly after this realization she went back to opiates (morphine this time) for another two and a half months. During the third month of her pregnancy she o.d.'d (overdosed) and went to a hospital, where she stayed 5 days and was detoxified. After the hospitalization she went to Florida with her child's father, where she remained drug free for 9 months. She used pills occasionally at this time.

> Three months after her child's birth she returned home and began using heroin. She used heroin for 4 months, then caught hepatitis and went to the hospital for two weeks, where she was detoxified. After this hospitalization she stayed off all drugs for 4 months while she lived with the child's father a third time. The child's father was not a drug user.

12. While it is true that persons do occasionally use drugs in prison and treatment, they seldom become physically addicted there.

Returning home to her family, where her two addicted brothers lived, after a fight with the boyfriend, she resumed use of heroin and barbiturates and continued to use them for 16 months. She described this period:

> I tried not to let my habit get too big. I would use for 5 or 6 days then stay off for a day using barbiturates. That way I could get high and not use too much stuff. Generally, if I didn't use heroin I would use pills or dollies.

Again she detoxified herself, this time with dollies, and was off heroin for one month. Near the end of this period she was arrested as an accomplice in a burglary and spent two months in jail. Rather than face the charges, she chose civil certification in the state program. At the time of the interview (December 1969) she had been in Manhattan Rehabilitation for 6 months.

At the time of the interview 58 months had elapsed since her initiation to opiates. Two-thirds (34) of those 58 months were spent using opiates, another 8 were spent in jail and treatment, and 16 were spent opiate-free on 4 different occasions.

I expect that many addicts have similar histories, with numerous periods of abstention both in and out of institutions, but they have not been documented in any systematic way. Certainly there are persons who use heroin for long and uninterrupted stretches, but they are those who have considerable money or are successful heroin sellers who avoid arrest and incarceration—they are not the usual street addict.

SUMMARY

How then do persons become addicted? It is most certainly a combination of social events operating within a cultural milieu that encourages drug use. Despite society's disdain for certain drugs we are a drug-taking culture. Evidence of this is all around us. Sociologist Hugh Parry found in two national samples that nearly half of the United States adult population reported the use of psychotropic drugs (sedatives, tranquilizers, and stimulants) at some time and that one-quarter was currently (1967) using one or more such drugs.[13] The mass media bombard us with encouragements to use drugs: television and radio commercials tell us to take Compoz for our nerves, Nytol for our insomnia, and, until recently, tobacco for myriad frustrations; magazines offer us alcohol of all varieties.

Doctors prescribe miracle drugs for anything from infection to

13. Hugh J. Parry, "Use of Psychotropic Drugs by U.S. Adults," in *Public Health Reports,* Vol. 83 (1968).

mental illness. The effects of many of these drugs are like magic—the drug may assist the body to fight off infection in a matter of hours, and former long-term psychotic patients leave hospitals where earlier it was thought they would remain for the rest of their lives. In 1969 pharmacists in the United States filled more than 202 million prescriptions for a variety of tranquilizers, energizers, amphetamines, barbiturates, and hypnotics.[14] Nearly two out of every five were new prescriptions; the rest were refills. This figure does not include those given and used in hospitals and clinics, which would raise this total considerably.

Drug companies manufacture thousands of tons of drugs each year and spend millions of dollars a year to promote their sale and use. Pierre Garai, a medical writer, estimates:

> Three-quarters of a *billion* dollars are spent yearly by some sixty drug companies to reach, persuade, cajole, pamper, outwit, and sell one of America's smallest markets, the 180,000 physicians. . . .[15]

The drug companies' object in these campaigns is to sell drugs—and they do. Henry Lennard and his associates, in their most interesting book *Mystification and Drug Misuse,* said:

> Most pharmaceutical firms have experienced substantial growth since the early 1950's. For example, in 1951, one company reported net sales of 9.5 million dollars; by 1970, this sales figure had reached 83.6 million dollars. Among the principal products of this company are central nervous [sic.] stimulants (amphetamines and amphetamine-barbiturate combinations) and antipsychotic agents (phenothiasine compounds). While the sale of all drugs has increased greatly for the industry as a whole, the sale of psychoactive drugs has increased to a greater extent.[16]

Medicine cabinets in most homes in the United States are a veritable cornucopia of prescription and nonprescription drugs. Drugs are a part of our everyday life and an integral part of not only the youth culture but that of adults as well. We are a drug-taking culture.

Beginning heroin use arises in group situations and out of associations with other drug users. Before persons try heroin they usually have taken marijuana or other drugs and are curious to

14. See M. Balter's address to the American Public Health Association, Houston, Texas, in October 1970.

15. Quoted in S. Malitz, "Psychopharmacology: A Cultural Approach," in *Symposium: Non-Narcotic Drug Dependency and Addiction,* Proceedings of the New York County District Branch, American Psychiatric Association, March 10, 1966.

16. Henry L. Lennard and associates, *Mystification and Drug Misuse* (San Francisco: Jossey-Bass, Inc., 1971).

experiment with still others. Often they know heroin users or addicts personally and learn from them, in glorified terms, the effects of heroin.

The social pressures of peer groups are well known to all of us, not only to sociologists. These pressures influence our vote, they encourage us to smoke, to drink, to overachieve, to underachieve, what have you. When the climate of the peer group (and most young people find themselves in such groups, however tightly or loosely organized) is to use or abuse illegal drugs, then this behavior is expected of each member of the group, like the one-time beer drinking of college freshmen, the street gang's recruitment of warriors for "bopping" (fighting), and the ways workmen prescribe how much work can be done on the assembly line. To resist is difficult; no one wants to be considered afraid to try drugs, a party poop, yellow, or a "rate buster."

And so a boy or girl tries heroin and, as with most drugs, the initial experience is a pleasing one, most especially with heroin. Using heroin once will not result in addiction. Confident of his power to control his life and destiny, the individual believes that he can control his drug use; he tries the drug again and again. In some respects the very effect of heroin supports this confidence of the user and encourages an inviolable attitude toward life. Alexander Trocchi, in his brilliant autobiographical novel, *Cain's Book,* describes these effects in a particularly revealing way:

> The mind under heroin evades perception as it does ordinarily; one is aware only of contents. But the whole way of posing the question, of dividing the mind from what it's aware of, is fruitless. Nor is it that the objects of perception are intrusive in an electric way as they are under mescalin or lysergic acid, nor that things strike one with more intensity or in a more enchanted or detailed way as I have sometimes experienced under marijuana; it is that the perceiving turns inward, the eyelids droop, the blood is aware of itself, a slow phosphorescence in all the fabric of flesh and bone; it is that the organism has a sense of being intact and unbrittle, and, above all *inviolable.* For the attitude born of this sense of inviolability some Americans have used the word "cool." [17]

Other people, other drug users, are necessary for getting and administering the drug, and the novice returns to those who provide the drug and the information about its use. As these associations develop the beginning user may find that he gets certain comfort in these associations as well as in the drug. They are often people like

17. Alexander Trocchi, *Cain's Book* (New York: Grove Press, Inc., 1960).

himself and they provide an atmosphere in which to talk about and discuss his drug experiences and, perhaps, a certain identity that he did not have before, that of a drug user.

After repeated use of heroin, usually but not necessarily over an extended period, the abuse of the drug becomes a habituation without actual physical dependence. This does not necessarily require everyday use, but perhaps some regular or habitual use, as on weekends. Jazz musicians in the 1950s called this, interestingly, an "ice cream habit."

This habituation may result from a number of psychological or sociological motives, as Isidor Chein et al. have described in their work *The Road to H.*[18] The abuser may use the drug because it eases certain anxieties and tensions he may feel; it may allow him to feel more confident as a person, to communicate and get along with others. (More than once male addicts have told me that they used heroin because it helped them to talk with girls.) Some use it to manage frightening hallucinations or paranoid thoughts that otherwise would cause considerable anxiety.

It may be used because one wants to be accepted socially by an important group in his life. He or she wants to belong and this is one way of doing it. It is often difficult to go against the tide, to be independent of the pressures of other people. New members of nearly any social group do things to ingratiate themselves with the others, and so might a youngster use heroin to show that he wants to be a part of what's happening and do what the group is doing.

Another reason might arise out of some need to establish a social identity—to be somebody, something. Establishing oneself—acquiring an identity—is difficult in our society; there are few effective rites of passage and very few institutional mechanisms to ease one into adulthood. As a consequence, some persons never make it, never feel adequate to the task, or do so only with considerable pain and anguish. For some the social identity of a heroin user may fill this void. It may be an identity despised by society, but it is nonetheless an identity.

Heroin use may also be part of a vocation. Drug sellers at levels above the street pusher can and do make money, and persons growing up in New York ghettoes know this. If one finds a good source of drugs that have not been too often diluted, there is an opportunity to make considerable money; this, in turn, can bring desired

18. For a much more extensive discussion of the motives for drug use, see this and other writings of psychologist Isidor Chein listed in the bibliography.

material objects, women and a certain status among addicts and, perhaps, the larger community.

Lastly, the habitué may use the drug as an act of rebellion against his family or society. Feeling frustrated by an overwhelming family, which may not allow him to conduct his life on his own terms, or by an irrational society that inculcates a need to achieve but blocks his opportunity, he lashes out against that which frustrates him. That the action of becoming a heroin user will not result in either the desired freedom or the chance for achievement is often of little moment to the individual; he acts out of a certain desperation in the only way he knows.

Obviously, there are few pure or simple motives for becoming habituated to heroin. In the complexity of human behavior there are also complex motives. Persons may rebel against their families and at the same time seek a vocation; they may both use heroin to ease their tensions and wish to be part of a group of people. The possible combinations of motives are innumerable.

After habituation to heroin, physical addiction soon follows. Now the abuser's need is not just psychological or social but physical as well. Now when he does not give himself regular and sufficient dosages he experiences withdrawal symptoms. It is now important to avoid withdrawal sickness, which becomes, perhaps, as important a motive as any of the others he may have for using drugs. Withdrawal symptoms abate in a matter of minutes after injection of heroin—magically the addict is well or high again, where moments before he was sick. The motives for using heroin become compounded; the physical gives reinforcement to the earlier psychological and social motives for habituation, and vice versa.

Without a steady supply of drugs the addict may experience one or more times a day a dehabilitating cycle of being sick one moment and high the next. Most, if not all, of his actions are oriented toward seeking drugs. Soon all of life has an overwhelming purpose and focus. Life is simplified into a single, engrossing need that must be met before consideration can be given to any of the other physical or social needs that we think are necessary for any reasonable life. Nearly all activity is focused upon the day-to-day struggle to get the drug to satisfy a single need. It is as if T. S. Eliot had been talking about addicts when, in his poem "The Love Song of J. Alfred Prufock," Prufock would like to roll the universe into a single ball. It would seem that addicts do roll their lives and the universe into such a ball, the single ball of heroin.

[3]

Supporting
a Habit

The development of increasing tolerance and the tendency of most urban addicts to attempt to replicate their original high causes them to use more and more heroin. Initially a user can get high on just a small amount; two or three will share a single bag. But gradually the dosage has to be increased in order to continue the euphoric effects. More than six out of ten persons (63%) reported that they used more than 20 bags a week. One particularly successful pusher told me that during one heroin run he had used 15 to 20 $5 bags a day every day for two months.

Along with the development of tolerance, the price of getting high or just supporting a habit escalates as well. At first getting high is relatively cheap, much cheaper than alcohol, but soon it costs more and more. Hore than half (59%) of the men in our samples reported that they spent more than $90 a week for drugs prior to going to treatment; three out of every ten (30%) reported that they spent $200 or more a week. Heroin addiction is indeed expensive, but not as expensive as those with a vested interest in drug treatment or enforcement would have us believe. In general our figures are considerably lower than the gross estimates of law-enforcement agencies, as printed by the press, and even those presented by the New York State Narcotic Addiction Control Commission.[1]

1. The Commission obtained information on daily cost and reported in their First Annual Statistical Report a median daily cost of $22.51 for 3,380 persons certified to their program. From this you get a weekly figure of $157, which is higher than our figure of $125.

Whatever the estimates, the cost of addiction is high, and if an addict neither is rich nor has some special attribute or skill for which society will pay large sums of money, then he inevitably will run out of money or exhaust his legal means of support. When this happens he will suffer some disruption in his education or legitimate work life.

Many doctors, musicians, and entertainers fall into the rich or skilled category. Bill Stern, the sportscaster; writer Alexander King; jazz musicians Charlie Parker, Lester Young, and Ray Charles; singers Billie Holiday and Janis Joplin; entertainer Lenny Bruce; novelists William Burroughs and Alexander Trocchi; all were or are currently able to lead relatively stable, productive lives despite their addiction.

Very few in our sample qualified as rich, skilled, or talented. Only a small percentage were able to complete their education; more than four out of five (86%) were school dropouts. Many of these dropped out of school before their heroin use for what may have been a variety of socioeconomic reasons that have been documented elsewhere,[2] but more than one in four (28%) dropped out because of drug abuse. This was particularly true of the youngest persons we interviewed, those 21 and younger. As the trend is for earlier and earlier addiction in New York, one may expect that more and more persons will be leaving schools as a result of drug abuse.

Without sufficient education, to say nothing of other disadvantages that result from poverty and racial discrimination, the opportunity for meaningful, well-paid, legitimate work is remote. Compound this with drug abuse and there is more disruption; three out of every five (59%) of the men in our sample reported that they had either lost or left their best or longest-held jobs because of drug abuse. Some addicts really intend to work, but when they start to experience severe and protracted withdrawal sickness they abandon work to seek the drugs they need. Seeking drugs becomes an all-consuming activity; if a job cannot offer immediate money to purchase drugs, then the addict is liable to toss it over for more immediately profitable pursuits.

Some addicts do manage to lead stable, legitimate work lives while using heroin, but they are few—so few in fact that we did not attempt to gather quantitative data about them. I did, however,

2. See Kenneth Clark's fine book about Harlem, *Dark Ghetto* (New York: Harper and Row, Publishers, 1965).

talk to two persons, both at Manhattan State Hospital, who worked throughout the full course of their addiction. Both were white. The first was Tony, a large, muscular Italian:

> I'm an over-the-road truck driver—you know, on a big rig, back and forth across the country. I made good money last year—$16,000. It's true that most of it went for dope, but I always managed to keep working. I had a good connection up in East New York in Brooklyn and I could always get enough to hold me. While I was driving I would just stay straight—just enough to let me function. When I would stop-over at night I'd get high. I did that for five years. Not that I didn't do a little hustling, too, 'cause I did, but I could always manage things without stealing or dealing dope too much. You know, if you steal or deal you're going to get caught eventually. Your chances just run out. Dealing's worse than stealing; those narcos are pretty fast runners.
>
> How did I get in here? My wife and my family made me volunteer. It got to be too much of a hassle just keeping them off my back.

Edward was a good-looking, fast talking Irishman:

> I was a window dresser. I worked in small department stores and shops all over the city, all up and down the East Coast. I have even gone into the Midwest as far as Kansas City. I've never really had to hustle really seriously. I've done a little on the side 'cause I always work and work steady. I've been using dope eight years and I've never been busted once. Generally, I could come up with enough bread to get a good stash. I might sell a little to friends, but I made sure I kept enough for myself.

For the majority of our sample work became nearly impossible after their addiction since most could never earn enough in a legitimate job to support their ever increasing habits. But even when an addict can work there is another obstacle to it, the dismissal by most addict groups of work as being square and devoid of meaning. Often in interviews with addicts I have thought that this antiwork attitude was a sour-grapes defense because so few have had meaningful work experiences and many do not consider good-paying or creative jobs work, but I think that these attitudes are more than psychological mechanisms. They are, I believe, deeper in the fabric of our society and arise out of poverty and the reality of poor, uneducated persons who can only expect to get the most dull, stultifying, and meaningless work. Most, I would expect, held these attitudes before their addiction and when they became addicted simply added another good reason not to pursue something that offered so little.

HUSTLING

The alternative to legitimate work for the urban addict is hustling, with its variety of activities. The term "hustling," as used by New York addicts, is much broader than that defined in Ned Polsky's brilliant study of the poolroom hustler, *Hustlers, Beats and Others*. Polsky's term is used to describe the activities of the men who earn their living by betting on different types of pool and billiard games. His definition of the term is a classic one, predating its use in describing prostitution, and is more restricted than the definition used by New York addicts.

Hustling, as the term is used by the persons of our sample, means any activity that utilizes guile or deceit to gain money. This may be either legal or illegal, but most often it is illegal. The specific activities may range from selling drugs at a wholesale level to petty thievery such as stealing from automobiles.

Selling Drugs

The best hustle for a narcotics addict is selling drugs, especially heroin. Not surprisingly, a large number do sell drugs as a principle means of support—one in three (33%) of our sample did so. These are, however, persons who specialize. Another 48% did not support their habits solely by selling drugs but did sell drugs or act as couriers for other drug sellers at some time during their drug careers. In all, eight out of ten (81%) of all those in our sample had sold drugs or acted as couriers and transported drugs at some time during their heroin use.

There are four principal kinds of drug sellers in New York. These are distinguished primarily by the margin of profits of their selling activity and by the quality and quantity of the drug they sell. Because there is no real consensus among addicts about their names, I will call them arbitrarily pushers, dealers, ounce or kilo connections, and, lastly, importers. By far the major part of drug selling is that done by a pusher for a small profit. The pusher is in nearly all cases an addict or user who buys a small quantity of heavily diluted heroin in three possible measures:

√ A "spoon," of varying size but usually a teaspoon

√ A "bundle," which consists of 25 or 30 $5 bags and a "half-bundle" of 15 $5 bags

√ A "load," which is 25 or 30 $2 bags and a "half-load" of 15 $2 bags

Sales are generally made to friends or close associates or persons accompanied by friends or associates. Depending upon a widely fluctuating market, the usual resale price for a single $2 bag is $3 and for a single $5 bag, from $5 to $7. With the purchase of two or more bags, the price may be reduced. Often the seller will either dilute or take a small quantity out of each bag before he sells it, either for resale or for his own use. The cost to the pusher of each of the quantities is approximately:

√ $25 for a spoon
√ $30–$45 for a half-bundle
√ $80–$90 for a bundle
√ $25–$30 for a half-load
√ $45–$60 for a load

The margin of profit is very small at this level. Let us assume that a pusher buys a load (30 $2 bags) for $50, uses 5 bags himself, and sells the remaining 25 bags for $60. The margin of profit is then only $10, plus the 5 bags he has used himself. These transactions can be carried out in a short time—in a matter of minutes or an hour or so—and if the pusher is energetic or has a large enough habit he could make two or three such transactions during a day. Each transaction would net him a small profit and a small quantity of drugs for his own use, but however hard he worked he would never make money. In many ways drug sales at this level are like those made by a large number of marijuana sellers as described by Erich Goode in his article "The Marijuana Market." [3] Like the marijuana seller, sales are made primarily to friends for a very small profit.

At the next level is the dealer. He, like the pusher, is an addict, but his margin of profit is somewhat larger and the drugs he sells are purer and in greater quantities. During my visits to Phoenix House at Hart Island I met and became friends with one such dealer, Ralph. Portions of my interviews with him about drug selling will tell you something of this level of operation:

> You won't believe it how I got selling dope. I was 13 at the time; I wasn't into anything much at the time—into booze and a little

3. Erich Goode, "The Marijuana Market," in *Columbia University Forum*, Vol. 12, no. 4 (1969).

smoke. Well, one day I was on the roof and I saw this dude come and hide something. It was his stash and there must have been 15 to 16 ounces of the best dope around. I found it and only had a vague idea of what it was; my buddy knew better than I, though. I started selling that dope in small match boxes for $5 a box. It was the best stuff around and everyone came back for more. The money was good and I used some of it to buy more dope. I sold dope on and off for about 6 months because I wasn't using it at the time myself. Eventually I tried it and used it every day after the first time. . . .

When I got hooked I was dealing all the time then. I started out buying a piece (an ounce); it would cost me about $500. By the time I got it it was cut 5 or 6 to 1—1 part heroin and 5 or 6 parts of benita (milk sugar) and quinine. I'd take it and cut it again; I'd add 5 ounces of benita to the original ounce making it 6 ounces. You got to be careful how you cut it—quinine eats up the dope so you got to put in plenty of benita. Benita is good because it dissolves easily. I'd then bag the lot; put it in $2 bags (this was in the South Bronx) and sell it for $30 a half-load. I got about 40 to 45 half-loads out of the original ounce. I would unload it in about four hours and make $500 to $600 over the initial $500 to buy the ounce. A couple of days later I would buy some more and do the same thing. . . .

The biggest I ever bought was an eighth of a kilo; it cost me $3,000. I got that from an Italian, but I used to buy from everybody—black, Italians, and a couple of Cubans. . . . None of these guys used dope themselves, not at that level. . . . I never bought in drug neighborhoods, always in classy neighborhoods in Long Island, Queens, and Manhattan on the East Side. I usually sold in the South Bronx and Harlem. . . .

Sometimes I got stuff on consignment—say when I'd just got out of jail. I was busted four times—three misdemeanors and a felony; twice by the narcos and twice by the police. I gave a narco $800 once to bust the charge down from a felony to a misdemeanor. I always tried to stay out of the streets; I'd lay up in my place or set up in a lieutenant's place. All of the contacts and sales were personal. We would use telephones, bars, and pick up things in drops all over the city. I always had a couple of people with me (addicts themselves); there was too much money involved to do it by myself. Even then I was taken off once—two of the guys with me got shot and the dope fiends got away with the dope. I looked for those guys for months after, but never found them. . . .

I was into other things as well. We stuck up payrolls now and then. I guess I did about 6 of these—the best was $8,000 and the lowest was $3,000. I was into fast figures on the numbers runners too; one of my boys was a numbers runner and he and I would get together with different people to do the policy bankers. It was pretty dumb when you think about it; if they had caught us they would have done us in.

As far as it was determinable, none of the persons I talked to in any of our samples were connections or importers. Dealers I talked with who had knowledge of these levels of drug sales said that few, if any, of the connections or importers were heroin users themselves. They may employ heroin users as testers to ascertain the purity of their supplies and to help them cut the drug, but they themselves do not use heroin. This seems to be borne out by reports from various police agencies and newspapers that persons arrested for possession or sales of large quantities of good quality opiates range over a broad spectrum of occupations—from diplomats to petty thieves—but they are not addicts.

There was, to say the least, considerable reluctance on the part of dealers to discuss connections and importers. They are known to most addicts and dealers alike as "the people," the Mafia, and few persons have first-hand knowledge of these operations. From what the police say the Mafia, while it has given up direct dealings with heroin at the large wholesale levels (supposedly as a result of their Appalachian conference), it has not given up the business completely. Instead of direct wholesaling they now "bankroll" (finance) the importation of heroin and leave the more dangerous wholesaling and distribution to others.

The new patterns of importation of heroin into the United States on the East Coast support this idea. Previously the importing route of opiates from their original sources in the Middle East, usually Turkey, to the United States was through Marseilles, where they were processed into heroin and then either smuggled directly into the United States or sent to Italy and from there to the United States. The new route seems to be through South America. Recent newspaper reports of large heroin and cocaine arrests have involved more and more Cubans and South Americans arriving in the United States from South America. These are, however, the ones who are apprehended; there are many, many more who are not caught—as evidenced by the large amount of heroin on the streets of New York. During the two years of the study there was not a single large-scale heroin panic in New York. There might have been small, local panics, but no such panics as have been witnessed previously in New York (the worst was in November of 1961) and certainly nothing like the scarcity of marijuana during the Spring and Summer of 1969 as a result of President Nixon's efforts with the Mexican government.

Most of the small-scale transactions of heroin occur within three communities in New York City—Central Harlem, South Bronx, and Bedford-Stuyvesant. All three are impoverished, black ghettoes that contribute large numbers of addicts to New York's

addict population. According to the folklore of addicts (not only in
New York but also in such far-ranging states as California and Ari-
zona) the best heroin in America—in quality and price—is found in
Harlem. This is certainly borne out by the prices of heroin in and
around New York; the lowest prices are found in Central Harlem,
where standards and prices for the different bags of heroin are established. A $5 bag bought in Harlem will bring $7 in Greenwich
Village and from $8 to $10 in other white Manhattan neighborhoods. Fifty miles away in Kingston, New York, the price is $15 to
$25. Persons as far away as Albany, New York, make regular shop-
ping trips to Harlem to purchase drugs.

The relatively good quality and low prices of heroin in black
communities give drug sellers in these places an advantage. More
blacks than either whites or Puerto Ricans reported that their
principal hustle to support their habit was selling drugs—41%, as
compared to 31% of the Puerto Ricans and 24% of the whites of
our sample. Whites, as they tend to live in less impoverished areas
that are farther from the principal drug markets, are less often spe-
cialists in drug sales. That is not to say that whites do not sell drugs,
for they do. Nearly as many whites as blacks reported that they had
at some time sold drugs, but far fewer reported that it was their
principal hustle.[4]

Stealing

On the other hand, more whites and Puerto Ricans (46% and
44%, respectively) reported that their principal hustle was stealing
than did blacks (35%). However, there was little or no difference
in the percentages of the three groups who said that they had stolen
at some time since their heroin use. Stealing for addicts encompasses
a broad range of activities—from stealing the family TV set to elaborate, well-planned payroll holdups. The most recurrent types of
stealing are shop-lifting, burglary, and street holdups (muggings or
rip-offs). Most often addict-thiefs will steal randomly, whatever they
can, whenever they can—stealing one day from cars, the next day
purses from old ladies, and the next from other addicts.

There are, however, a good number of skilled and imaginative
specialties. One of the more amusing specialties in New York is that
of the *cattle rustler*. The rustler makes a regular practice of stealing

4. For another description of drug selling in New York see Edward
Prebble and John H. Casey's fine article "Taking Care of Business—The Heroin
User's Life on the Street," in *The International Journal of the Addictions*,
Vol. 4, no. 1 (1969).

meat from large supermarkets and reselling it to neighbors in his local community. Wearing a large overcoat, he goes to a supermarket and steals choice cuts of packaged meats—T-bone and sirloin steaks, roasts, legs of lamb, and, if the community is Italian, veal— and secretes them in his overcoat while he buys one or two items of insignificant value. Once out of the store he goes from door to door, selling the meat at a reduced price. Surprisingly, there is a large market for such obviously stolen goods in many poor communities. A good cattle-rustler may go to several supermarkets a day and have a regular group of customers. It is not uncommon for housewives even to place orders for special cuts of meat.

Another interesting specialty was that of Roger, a white addict of six years, who said that he worked only on Friday:

> Every Friday, about lunch time or after, I would dress up and go down to the large office buildings in the garment district carrying a shopping bag from one of the expensive department stores. I would then go from office to office asking directions, or asking to borrow a pencil, whatever came into my head, and pick up any purse or pocketbook I could get my hands on. The purse went into the shopping bag, and I would thank the secretary or typist politely and leave the office. As soon as I got out of the office I would go up to the next floor, go into the john, clean out the purse—money, I.D.'s and credit cards—and stuff it in the trash basket. I'd then go down on the elevator and go to the next building and do the same thing. I'd get four or five in a day and could hustle $300 or $400. Most times I would get cash, but if it was a check I'd get someone to take it to a check-cashing place (using the I.D. in the purse) and split it. You can't believe how it worked. I got enough every Friday to go through the whole week; that way I wouldn't heat up any one place too much.

Another hustle that requires considerable skill and the ability to manipulate persons is short-changing:

> Let me tell you how we did it. I guess there is a lot of ways to do it, but this one really works. You can beat three or four out of five you try. Go into a store with a $20 bill and four or five single dollars and buy something for less than a dollar. Pay with the $20 bill.
>
> As the clerk is counting out your change ($19 plus change) you say, "I've got a lot of singles here—have you got $10 for ten singles (or $5 and five singles)?" Getting in your purse you pull out five singles and take the four singles he has already given you and give him back $9 for a $10 bill.
>
> He then counts the nine bills and says, "Hey, you only gave me $9." Acting nonchalant you say, "Yes, you're right. Here is $1—will you give me a $20 bill instead. Here is $10." Then you give him back the $10 he has just given you for the ten singles.

By that time he is so confused and flustered that more than likely he will give you the $20 bill. And you just beat him out of $10. That's all you do is get them so confused you can just tell them what to do. If he is quick enough he will pick up on it, and if he does you apologize and claim it was an honest error.

One time there was three of us went across the States to Michigan, short-changing all the way. We must have hit half the stores and gas stations on the way. We'd get $200 to $250 a day.

I only got caught once—that was in a gas station upstate. Then I just acted innocent, and the guy let me off when I gave him the money back. Generally you can only get away with it once, but if they are real dumb you can try it twice. Usually they don't find out about the mistake until they count up the till. By that time you are long gone. I guess I must have beat a couple thousand people with that one. It works all the time.

Burglary figures large in the addict's repertory of stealing. Although we did not collect any quantitative data on the frequency of the various specialties of stealing it would seem from police statistics on arrest that burglary ranks along with shop-lifting as one of the more recurrent specialties. Both guile and skill figure in burglary, but often the addict's need for drugs will drive him to commit daring and even foolhardy thefts. An acquaintance told me a story that illustrates the guile of one such addict-burglar:

I'd just got home from work, taken off my clothes (it was a hot, muggy day), and was sitting in a large chair in the sitting room having a drink, reading a newspaper, and intermittently watching the news on TV. I heard a noise in the bedroom and peered down the hall into the bedroom (it was about 25 or 30 feet from where I was sitting) and saw the reflection of a young, black man in the mirror over the chest of drawers. It didn't register right away, I guess; I was too surprised by it. When I finally put it together, I got up and ran into the bedroom. By that time the boy had gone out the window and was going down the fire escape. I yelled something down the fire escape and then went to call the police.

The boy must have been in that bedroom at least five or ten minutes while I was in the sitting room and my wife was in the kitchen. He went through the drawers of the dresser taking jewelry and cash and then went through my suits and pants pockets. He made off with about $150 in cash and $250 in jewelry.

Yes, he was an addict. It seems he stumbled or something going down the fire escape and sprained his leg. A cop happened by at the time and picked him up as he tried to hurry away. The same night I identified the jewelry at the precinct; I really couldn't have identified the boy, because I didn't see him all that well. He must have been really driven to attempt that robbery while we were in the apartment. Especially in our apartment, which is pretty small.

Much more polished and adept was the technique of Dave, who at 19 was a skilled cat burglar:

> I learned everything I know from a locksmith-burglar who I used to pal with. He really knew what he was doing; there isn't a lock made that he can't get to. We used to work Rego Park and Forest Hills in Queens. We'd go to a big apartment high-rise during the day dressed like delivery men. We'd go up the elevator, ring the door bell, and if no one answered go to work on the lock tumbler. We had this tool that would just pull the tumbler right out.

> We'd open up the door and then pull the door shut with the tumbler jammed in. If someone came to the door on the outside, they couldn't open the door, no way. Well, we'd clean out the place—cash, jewelry, silver, TV and hi-fi sets. If there was no doorman we would just come down on the elevator with the whole lot—put all the small, loose stuff in a suitcase we picked up in the apartment. If there was a doorman, we'd go down the fire escape. Sometimes we would hit two or three places in the same building in an afternoon. We'd stash the whole lot in a panel truck and then take it over to a fence.

Most addict-burglars attempt to get cash or items that are easily sold or pawned—radios, color television sets, hi-fidelity equipment, and the like. Sale of the items may be made to fences, but often the individual will sell them himself to persons in his local neighborhood. Nonaddicts who live in the addict's community are often willing accomplices to his thefts. They buy expensive items at a fraction of their original purchase price and knowingly support the addict in his efforts to secure his needed drugs.

Prostitution and Pimping

After theft, the next most prevalent hustles are activities that have to do with sex—prostitution, both male and female, and pimping. Prostitution for women is a common means of supporting a habit but not necessarily the primary means of support. Surprisingly, as many women reported that they sold drugs (27%) as a principal means of supporting their habits as reported prostitution (26%), and a nearly equal number said that they stole (22%) to support their habits. Many women have resorted to part-time or occasional prostitution at various times in their addict careers without the activity becoming a major means of support; in addition to the 27% who said it was their principal hustle, another 18% reported some prostitution during their addict careers. Rita, an attractive 23-year-old Puerto Rican girl, was such a part-time prostitute:

> While I was using stuff (heroin) I managed to live pretty well, about like you straights. I worked all the time—sewing up pocketbooks in

the garment district. I had my son with me all the time, I ate every day, went to Orchard Beach in the summertime, and visited my mother in Puerto Rico every year.

The way to do it is turn a few tricks regularly. I never stood on no corners. I had a couple of regular guys that used to come every weekend. I'd maybe do three or four a day on Saturday or Sunday and pick up $75 or $100. My regulars were always good to me—one gave me $50 once. I like hustling. I don't like the people—some are real creeps—but I like the money.

Rita is something of an exception in her ability to live a reasonable life and function well as a person while addicted, but her part-time casual hustling is not exceptional. Many women and girls drift in and out of hustling as they need money or as different opportunities for other hustles arise. Prostitution is treated matter-of-factly; it is a good and easy way to make money.

More in line with the public image of the female addict-prostitute are the experiences of Jeanne, a very vivacious, talkative, 19-year-old black girl, and Marie, a voluptuous but tired looking woman of 21 years. Jeanne is first:

After I got strung out, I left home to live with this beautiful dude in Jamaica, Long Island. He was a big-time dealer, mostly in heroin and coke. He didn't use stuff himself. Oh, he used a little bit of coke now and again, but he didn't use stuff at all. Well, I was living up there in this big house with my partners, two girls I knew on the streets. All of us were dope fiends. His place was something of an after-hours joint; like a club, but nothing like a bar. All three of us was waitresses and ran the bar.

There was a bunch of crooks and underworlders used to hang out all the time and Archie ask us to go with them. It was just a little drawer money for him and we got dope from the dudes. I just started out easy like that. I was always high so I didn't mind. None of them meant anything to me—they was just tricks.

Well, that was cool till Archie kicked me out—then I had to scramble on the streets. I was dealing a bit, for about a month, then I hit the streets. I used to work Brownsville and down at Atlantic Avenue and 4th in Brooklyn. We had a trick house set up where you paid the dude who run it $2 to use the room. I hung out in the bars and on the street. I worked it seven days a week for six months. I'd usually pull $50 a day; charge $7 to $10 a trick and do about 6 or 7 a night.

It's easy money, but I don't like it. You get a lot of freaks, weirdos. You got to protect your asshole. Like they always offering you more money. When I seed that things weren't correct, I'd just walk off and say, "I'll see you later, honey." I always carried a knife; you have to. If he came at me I'd get him [gesturing toward the groin]. I'd rather deal than hustle; it's too much of a hassle.

Marie's experience was much longer:

> I started hustling (prossing) about a month after I started using stuff.
> I was in Puerto Rico; I was sixteen then. I got strung out and I
> didn't know where to cop so I went to a friend. He told me what to
> do and I went into the streets. I made $100 the first week and shared
> it with my *unchulo* (pimp), who was an addict, too. He was good-
> looking and we were lovers, but I wasn't in love with him. You know
> what I mean?
>
> I did that for a year, then came to New York to get off drugs. I
> moved in with my family in Williamsburg. After a couple of months
> I was on to stuff again. I moved out of my family's house and moved
> in with my pimp; I was hustling again. I lived with the pimp just
> for dope and hustling; he was a friend only. I had a boyfriend at the
> time; he lived with us.
>
> In a good week I'd make $250 to $300; $40 a day for 6 or 7 tricks.
> A bad day would be $15, like when it rained or was cold. Most of
> the money went for dope. I paid the rent, bought candy and soda,
> and most of the dope for the three of us. My pimp would help me
> hustle tricks and my boyfriend would deal a little bit of dope.
>
> After a year I got busted for pross, did 15 days, and when I came out
> of the House of D [Detention] my pimp and my boyfriend were gone.
> So I got another pimp. I liked him; we had good times together.
> I worked Williamsburg and he sold dope. Now and then he'd get
> half a piece and push it. I usually brought in most of the money.
> We were together on and off for nine months.
>
> My fourth pimp was after the first time I was on aftercare [from Man-
> hattan Rehabilitation Center, where she had been returned for a
> second time]. I was living in Manhattan with a girlfriend down near
> Delancey Street. I met this guy that I liked and we turned on and got
> down together [had sexual intercourse]. I started living with him,
> using stuff everyday. Two weeks later I was hooked again and started
> hustling along Delancey and Rector Streets. We stayed together for
> six months. Sometimes we were happy, but I don't think I love him.
> He was selling a little. Once we bought half a piece but used most of
> it ourselves. I guess he wasn't a real pimp. It wasn't like he would
> get tricks, but he protected me and looked after me. That lasted until
> I was picked up on a warrant [for violating her aftercare].

Marie obviously likes the companionship of men. She gives a
good deal for this companionship; often she was the major contributor of the couple or group. She supplied the money for drugs,
paid the rent, and kept them in what little food they ate. The men
helped her with her trade, copped for her, and did a little minor
drug selling. Her "pimps" were of two types: two (the first and
second) were like the classic pimp—persons who helped her get
tricks and were actively involved in her work; two (the third and

fourth) were much more like a *pounce*—a man who serves more as a companion, lover, and protector than the pimp.

The merging of distinctions between the two types of pimp, as made by Marie, is a common one among women addicts. An addict-prostitute tends to view any male who lives with and, perhaps, off her as being "her pimp." Men, on the other hand, view the role of the pimp in its more classical sense. A pimp, according to male addicts, is someone who actively helps the prostitute to get tricks. Men who do *not* actively assist the prostitute do *not* consider themselves as pimps but more as lovers or boyfriends and, in some cases, husbands. Most men who live with or off prostitutes tend to keep a certain distance from her work. They do this by keeping their hand in other hustles—selling drugs in a minor way or petty thievery. In most of these relations the woman is the major contributor and brings in the most money and the man's contribution is a minor one. This is a reversal of the American ideal of the role of men and women. Such a reversal of the ideal carries with it considerable stigma; in many states it is against the law for a man to live off the earnings of a prostitute. Consequently, men who live with or off prostitutes try to avoid the label of pimp and are reluctant to admit the role, while women tend to label as "pimp" anyone who lives with or off them, whatever his relation to her work.

Very few men in our sample admitted to the role of full-time pimp. Only 3% of our total sample of men said that their principal hustle was pimping, but another 25% reported that they had at some time in their addict careers engaged in pimping. I would expect in both instances the frequency of under-reporting to be considerable. If I were to ask the question again, with my present hindsight, I would word it differently or perhaps devise two questions to cover the two types and in this way get around the male's reluctance to admit pimping.

Society's evaluation of prostitution and pimping is a strange, ambiguous one. It is at once accepted as necessary and despised. Men actively participate in it and yet moralize about it. They consort with prostitutes and at one and the same time abhor them. Society enacts laws to punish the prostitute and the pimp and then looks away from those who solicit their services.

Some of this attitude and behavior may be a result of our earlier Victorian conception of sex: women were not expected to enjoy sex but to participate out of duty. Women who liked sex were "bad"; "good" women did not admit to any sexual pleasure. Men, on the other hand, were baser animals, but held ambiguous attitudes about enjoying it and particularly about women who enjoyed it. Prostitutes, because they were supposed to enjoy sex, were considered bad; at the same time they excited the imagination of men and became for many men a regular source of pleasure. All prostitutes, addict or nonaddict, remain victims of these attitudes despite the current "sexual revolution."

Prostitution is in many ways a good occupation for addicts under our present irrational system of control. The hours are short, the money is good, and most young girls have a saleable commodity. The hazards are not as great as one would expect. New York police, except during "clean-up" campaigns, are reluctant to arrest prostitutes; judges are even more reluctant to convict them. Conviction brings small fines and very short jail sentences. (At the time of the study prostitution was considered only an offense in New York, but it was recently made a misdemeanor again.) Venereal disease, with the new drugs, is no real threat to anyone who knows the early symptoms and can act on them. The greatest hazards are the changes it causes in self-conception, but that is something that I will discuss more thoroughly in the chapter on women.

Homosexual prostitution, more specifically "sex with persons of the same sex for money," also figures in the hustling activities of addicts on a less regular and more casual basis. Both sexes report this activity; 28% of the males said they had had sex with men for money, while 23% of the females said they had had sex with women for money. Homosexual prostitution is not, however, a sustaining hustle—only 1% of both groups said it was their main hustle. More often than not this activity is not considered by the male addict as homosexual behavior. Men do not consider themselves as homosexuals simply because they have had sex with men. When money is received, there is seldom a label of homosexuality on the addict's part; it is seen as one of the many ways to procure money and has little to do with his sexual identification.

Women, perhaps because they have more opportunity for prostitution with the opposite sex, attach more stigma to homosexual prostitution; more seem to assume sexual identification from this activity than do men. Many more women addicts reported being homo- or bisexual than men (29% as compared to 3%; the men perhaps underreported). Not by any means, however, do all women define themselves as homosexuals because they have had sex with women. My observations are that women addicts as a group are more tolerant of homosexual activity than are male addicts; homosexual activity was much more prevalent in the female treatment facility (Manhattan Rehabilitation Center) in which we made our interviews than in the male facilities. Many more females actively engaged in homosexuality and talked about it than did men. It must, however, be made clear that many women at Manhattan Rehabilitation Center, when given a choice of sexuality, chose the opposite sex and were homosexual within that facility only out of a lack of choice. These women were similar to the "jail-house turnout" described by Gene Katzenbaum in *Women's Prison,* a book about Fontana, a California women's prison. The jail-house turnout is a woman who engages in homosexual activity while in prison but is heterosexual on the outside.

Running Numbers

Working with the policy rackets is also an occasional source of funds for the addict but seldom a regular, steady activity. More than a quarter (26%) of the men said that they had "run numbers" at some time during their heroin use, but only a few (3%) made enough or did it long enough to support a habit. Men who work in the policy rackets are reluctant to use known addicts in the business; they fear that the addict will run off with money and be generally unreliable. One addict with whom I spoke said that he had been a collector for three years but was able to do this only because very few people knew about his addiction and the only one who did that mattered was his brother. The temptation of handling rather large sums of money daily (the job is not unlike that of a bank teller) is probably too difficult for the addict, and policy racketeers know this from experience.

THE ADDICT PECKING ORDER

Prestige is just as important in the addict world as it is in the larger society. Just as work is one of the means of achieving prestige in straight society, so is hustling in the addict society. Actually there are few real differences between the ways in which both confer prestige and position; the basis is essentially the same in both. In hustling much depends upon whom you know, how you manage your personal relations with others, and certain skills in securing money and drugs and in avoiding the police.

Those with the best "rep" (greatest prestige) within the addict culture are the large drug sellers, the dealers.[5] In addition to wearing expensive clothes, driving large automobiles, and having available women (not unlike straight society's captains of industry), the drug dealer has a constant supply of drugs. Withdrawal symptoms are not a problem for him and he can get high any time he wants to. If drugs are no problem for him, the police are—as he is often the major focus of their efforts to control narcotics traffic. The drug dealer's principal concern is how to manage his day-to-day work and avoid scrutiny by the police. This requires considerable skill and a great deal of healthy paranoia. Money may assist him in this regard: it allows him to hire "lieutenants" who will assume the danger of handling the drug and transacting sales, to bribe a narcotics officer or policeman or make a deal to be indicted on a lesser charge, and to raise most bails set so that he will not have to go to jail for months prior to the actual trial. He is not, however, immune from the police or the courts; he doesn't deal with enough money to assure that.

Skilled burglars, thieves, and con men hold similarly high positions among addicts. These are the "good dope fiends," the "men" of the culture. Considerable skill and planning are utilized by this small but elite group. Often they buy drugs in relatively large quantities and sell them as well.

"Rip-off" thieves (crude and potentially violent men), shoplifters, purse snatchers, and muggers hold an intermediate status. Most of their criminal activity is committed out of an urgent and immediate need for drugs and is consequently done with little or no planning; they seize any opportunity to steal something or "take somebody off." The activity, while continual, is often random; it requires more nerve and guile than skill or brains.

Low men on the status ladder among addicts are those who possess neither skill nor guile. These are the ones who are always dependent upon others for money and drugs—who steal from their families continually, who "cop" (purchase) quantities of drugs for other users in exchange for part of a bag or who "lend their works for a taste." These are the incompetents, who are generally held in mild contempt by other, more competent addicts. Attitudes about the incompetent are illustrated in a discussion I had with one of the research assistants in the Harlem Hospital Methadone Maintenance

5. This does not necessarily include the kilo connection or trafficker from our earlier classification of drug sellers (though it could); so few addicts were in these classifications that I have not thought it necessary to discuss them here.

Clinic about the reliability of another patient's responses to a pilot interview I made:

> I've known that bastard for 10 years. He had to be the worst, greasiest dope fiend in Harlem. He couldn't even hustle his ass. He used to take off his old mother all the time; she's about 60. He'd meet her on the way home from the subway and steal her purse. The only dope he ever shot was out of the cottons [used to strain impurities].

A particularly good and faithful dramatization of the prestige heirarchy among addicts can be found in the play and movie *The Connection,* by Jack Gelber. All the statuses are represented—Cowboy, the high-status black dealer, dressed all in white; Solly, the competent "man" of the group; Ernie, the "rip-off" dreamer; and Leach, who lives off other addicts by making his "pad" available as a shooting gallery.

The position of women in the prestige hierarchy is more complex. Early in their careers they are often associated—as lover, girlfriend, or wife—with a competent addict. As in the larger society, the woman assumes the status of her lover or spouse and shares his success and spoils. Seldom is such a relationship long standing, however; the man eventually is arrested or suffers some other setback. When this happens, the woman is thrown upon her own resources. Her most available resource is her body, which she usually sells. If she is the least bit competent as a prostitute she gradually becomes independent of men—either forming loose alliances as Marie did in our earlier descriptions or, sometimes, living with other women either as friend or lover.

Most male addicts envy and disparage female addicts. They envy their ability to earn money easily by selling themselves. Men often feel that they have the worst of it; they feel that they are more susceptible to arrest and conviction than are women. Often they disparage women for doing the same things they do themselves. Employing the usual double standard, they expect that women should be more honorable, faithful, and loyal than they are themselves. When women do not live up to this ideal they "put them down." The female addict usually senses this male deprecation and moves either toward more independence or toward women. Not all women fit this pattern, but a good number do.

The reputation of an addict, or more formally his status and prestige, usually follows him while he is off the street in prison or treatment. Within prison certain deference is given to those with strong street reputations, not only by other prisoners, residents, or patients, but by guards and staff as well. This is true of self-help, therapeutic communities like Synanon as well; those with strong reputations on the street as competent addicts are often in jobs that have considerable prestige. I don't believe that there is any particular mystery in this; competent people, except in a society with a rigid caste system, are competent wherever they are.

HONOR AMONG ADDICTS

Contrary to the common belief about thieves and honor, there is little honor among addicts. Addicts are continually "taking each other off" (stealing money and dope from each other). Not unlike their relationships with family and friends, addicts continually use each other and seek any and all advantages. Friendship and family ties are often very thin where heroin is involved: brothers will steal from sisters, husbands from wives, long standing friends will inform upon each other to the narcotics police. The defense against being had by others is a vigilant, aggressive attitude and a willingness to carry and use a weapon. Most, if not all, New York addicts carry knives, and on occasions some carry guns.

An addict out of his "turf" (local community) where he is not known is considered ready game and must be particularly cautious about how he "carries himself" and whom he associates with. Some addicts specialize in taking off other addicts and preying upon strange persons in their neighborhood.

Paradoxically, heroin use—which begins in a social situation and continues during early use to be very social—becomes, after addiction, a more and more solitary, singular activity. After prolonged addiction it gets to be every man for himself; each is alone in his efforts to get drugs. Each must satisfy his own need for drugs before he can give any consideration to others. There are no rests, no vacations; the need is continual and must be met every day.

Hustling is both continual and solitary; the addict must work and work hard to get the price of drugs. He must work for his own need; there is not usually enough left for anyone else. He has to protect himself not only against society and the police but against other addicts who have just as strong a need as his own. In the end most addicts find themselves alone with their addiction—without family and friends, and with few associates.

[4]
It's Not All Getting High

What most people, professionals and laymen alike, don't realize about narcotic addicts is that most addicts, and particularly the young and short-term users, enjoy their experiences with heroin and wish to continue using it. They enjoy getting high; they enjoy the relative immunization to pain and anxiety that heroin gives them. Consequently, many are loath to give it up and only do so when the hazards of use or the pressures of society become so great that they are forced to.

Using heroin is not all getting high, though; there are a good number of hazards associated with its use: most of these are, for the most part, corollary to its use rather than a direct result of it. Actually, long-term heroin use without the experience of periodic withdrawal and taken under sterile conditions seems to have few deleterious effects on mental or bodily functions. As yet there is no evidence that prolonged use of heroin under the conditions mentioned above causes any major physical or mental deterioration. That is not to say that there are no hazards to heroin use for there are, but most arise out of the physical and social conditions of its use rather than its direct effects.

The major hazards of heroin use for addicts (in the United States) are the possibility of contracting hepatitis, the possibility of death resulting from an overdose, a general disregard for physical health because of focused drug-seeking behavior, and possible arrest and incarceration. None of these is a direct result of heroin itself; each is associated with its use because the addict lives in a society that defines him as a criminal and forces him to go to illegal sources for the drug and for instruments for its injection. Hepatitis results from unsterile and communal injection conditions (it is against the law to possess works); overdose, from the unknown quality of the drug (which has been bought illegally); and arrest and incarceration, from the high costs of illegal heroin and the existing federal and state laws that define its possession and sale as a crime.

Other hazards of heroin use are less clearly delineated but hazards nonetheless. The distinctions between sickness and health, life and death, freedom and incarceration are obvious. Less obvious are the kinds of behavior that many addicts employ and develop to exploit relationships—with friends, lovers and spouses, doctors, and so forth—to get money to buy drugs, and the long-term effects upon social relationships among family and friends to say nothing of the relationships between addicts and square society when they are under the prolonged effects of a powerful drug. The exploitive, manipulative behavior of addicts when seeking drugs has led many people who treat them, both professionals and paraprofessionals, to characterize them as being different or as having certain personalities that are distinct from nonaddicts. Leaders at Synanon and other self-help therapeutic communities have told me that they believe that addicts *are* different from nonaddicts. One director at the former San Francisco Synanon used an analogy of six fingers to describe addicts like himself:

> Addicts are like persons with six fingers on a hand; they are different from those with five. It took us a long time to realize that.

Similarly, the addict is said to have a character disorder or to be a psycho- or sociopath. All of these terms are used to describe, with a good deal of dismay, the tendency of addicts to relapse to heroin, and when they are addicted to manipulate persons and situations to help them seek and use drugs. They are, in effect, a stigmatization of the addict that society utilizes to disparage the addict and discourage drug use.

HEALTH HAZARDS

Serum hepatitis, a disease of the liver, is very prevalent among addicts. This disease is transmitted through the blood of an infected person. Originally it was believed that hepatitis was transmitted only by means of an infected injection needle, but recent evidence shows that injection is not a necessary precondition to infection. Injection is, however, a very effective way to transmit the blood from one person to another and spread the disease.

Few addicts under our system of control make any pretense of sanitary conditions for the injection of a drug they may use as often as four or five times a day. There are no attempts to sterilize the skin at the point of injection or to use sterile needles. To complicate matters, addicts often use a common needle, either among friends or in shooting galleries, passing it from person to person, so that the possibility of infection among a group of persons is often compounded. Nearly one out of four in our sample (23%) said they had had hepatitis at some time during their addict careers.

Despite a tendency toward hypochondria while off heroin, impoverished addicts show little, if any, regard for their health while on heroin and as a consequence are often in poor health during their heroin use. This may be attributed both to difficulties in getting the drug and to the analgesic power of the drug itself. Heroin, while relatively cheap for the beginning user, is very expensive for those who have developed a high tolerance for it, and such a tolerance is almost inevitable. It is not uncommon for addicts to use $20 to $30 a day for drugs; if every time you shoot up you have to use two or three bags just to avoid withdrawal symptoms, then heroin use can be very expensive. As a result of the very high costs of addiction, addicts tend to use all of whatever money they have for buying drugs; very little is used for food and shelter, to say nothing of health considerations. Often addicts will go without eating, except candy and soda, for days or weeks; during the summer months, rather than spend money on a room or apartment they will sleep on rooftops or in basements.

Heroin is a potent analgesic; when used with any regularity it masks symptoms of illness and disease that are easily detected in persons not using heroin. This was brought home to me during a conversation I had with a resident of Hart Island (Phoenix House). This is a transcription of that conversation:

> While I was riding on the ferry to Hart Island, I met Jerry T. coming back from pass. He was wearing a T-shirt and as I sat down next to him I noticed a violent, massive scar on his left arm from his shoulder to his elbow. We talked about it:
>
> D.W.: How did you get that terrible burn?
>
> J.T.: I was shooting dope at the time. I fell out [became unconscious because of an overdose of drugs] and fell up against a hot water pipe

in the bathroom. I must have laid up against it for 10 to 15 minutes. My old lady came and found me laying up against the pipe.

D.W.: You must have been in the hospital for some time with that one.

J.T.: Naw, I didn't even go to a doctor. I was high, man, high all the time. I didn't feel a damn thing. It took about a month to heal and I was high every moment of that month. I had a lot of shit then. Oh, my old lady put some water on it, but that was all.

Addicts in our sample reported major shifts in the state of their health while using heroin as compared to before its use and while they were in treatment. When asked, "Would you say your health was good while you were using heroin?" half (49%) said that it was *not* good during heroin use, while only one in twenty (6%) said their health was *not* good before heroin use. The response for the period during treatment was similar to that before heroin use —only 6% said their health was *not* good during both periods. Some of these reports may be of persons complaining of withdrawal symptoms during drug use, but the finding is supported by the clinical experiences of doctors.

OVERDOSE

Heroin, as it passes from its manufacturing source to the user on the street, is diluted any number of times—first by the importer, then by the connection, then by the dealer, and lastly by the pusher. The buyer in most instances does not know the strength of the drug without testing it; it could be anywhere from 3% pure, the strength of the usual bag of heroin, to 100% pure. He can only have a vague idea, as indicated in a gross way by color and texture.[1]

Because the quality of the drug is almost always unknown there is always a possibility of accidental overdose. This happens much more often than is generally thought. During the summer of 1970 there was a rash of deaths in New York City due to overdose, known medically as acute reaction to dosage or overdosage; 40 persons died in a single two-week period. The autopsies performed by the medical examiner showed no signs of disease or contaminants in the bodies. Death was in all cases due to "acute reaction"; one can only surmise that, perhaps, the victims had simply used a purer drug than they had reckoned on.

Another factor contributing to death from acute reaction is

1. Heroin in its purer form is often darker in color and more compact than it is in its street form.

the desire on the part of nearly all urban addicts to get high. Most heroin users are not content to be just straight, though that may be all they can afford; they prefer to be high. This desire to be high and the development of tolerance cause most addicts to increase their dosage steadily. As each person has a specific tolerance that may vary from day to day or week to week, it is difficult to determine the increment of increased dosage that will provide the desired high. Thus it is very easy to inject too much and fall out. More than half (53%) of our sample reported that they had at some time experienced an overdose and lost consciousness. Many had done this not once but several times. One Italian addict said that he fell out at least once a week during the three years that he used heroin:

> I only went to the hospital once through all of that. . . . No, I wasn't trying to kill myself—I just always wanted to be high. You know, being straight is not enough. There is no reason to use dope if you don't get high.

The effects of an overdose of heroin are well known to street addicts, and there are a good number of folk antidotes used to counter their effects, some of which have little relation to recognized medical treatment. These range from mouth-to-mouth resuscitation to injection of salt solutions to placing a packet of ice between the victim's legs, against the genitals. The last would, if anything, cause an effect contrary to the usual medical treatment to overcome the depressant effects of heroin on the central nervous system.

Dr. Milton Halpern, New York City's Chief Medical Examiner, has made a major study of death due to narcoticism (acute reactions and other related causes) and has found it is one of the principal causes of death among persons 15 to 35 years of age in New York City today—more than murder, suicide, accidents, and disease—and is increasing every year. During 1968, the year of our survey, there were 656 deaths due to narcoticism in all age groups, an increase of 110% over 1961, when 311 died from the same causes, and 719% over the 1951 figure of 80. The increase over a 17-year period was more than seven-fold.

The years 1969 and 1970 saw even greater increases in the number of deaths due to narcoticism; during 1969 the numbers increased to 1,011 but declined during 1970 to 866. (There was, however, in 1970 an increase in the number of addicts dying as a result of nondirect causes, that is homicides, suicides, accidents, etc.

Dr. Halpern's analysis showed:

> 1. The ratio of male victims to female victims in 1969 was the same as the proportion of male to female drug abusers known to the City

of New York Narcotics Registry—there were five male victims to every female. Since 1965 there has been a steady increase in the proportion of male victims to females when the ratio was 3:1.

2. The borough of Manhattan had the dubious honor of having the greatest number of deaths due to narcoticism (439 or 43% in 1969), but there has been a growing trend towards dispersal to other boroughs in New York over the last ten years. A decade previous (1959), 75% of the deaths due to narcoticism occurred in Manhattan.

3. Approximately 55% of the victims were black persons, 25% were white and 20% Puerto Rican, which is similar to the ethnic percentages of heroin abusers known to the Narcotics Registry in 1969.

4. By far the majority of deaths result from acute reactions of dosages or "overdose" though doctors do not in all cases know the precise mechanisms that cause such reactions to dosage. Most of the other cases were caused from unsterile injection procedures which resulted in hepatitis, tetanus, heart infections and brain damage.[2]

INCARCERATION

Another hazard to the addict's life that may be as dehabilitating as disease is the possibility of going to jail or prison as a result of what is obviously a medical condition. Since the Harrison Act of 1916 the addict in America has been defined as a criminal and until very recently has been treated like one in every state of the nation. Year by year, as citizens and law-makers have become more and more alarmed by an increasing consciousness of the problems of drug abuse and addiction, there have been increases in the policing of addicts and in the lengths of prison terms for possession and sale of drugs. Not surprisingly, the long-term effects of these laws have shown *little or no effect,* as argued by William Butler Eldridge in his fine study of the effectiveness of the laws of seven states (New York, New Jersey, Illinois, California, Michigan, Ohio, and Missouri) and Washington, D.C. He concluded:

> Five years ago the . . . [White House Conference on Drugs] found the nation committed to the promise that control of narcotic addiction and narcotic abuse depended upon a severe and repressive system of punishment—chiefly long prison terms without the possibility of probation or parole. This was the premise underlying the approach to all forms of narcotic violation—smuggling, selling, dispensing, possession, record keeping, treatment. The proponents have often said that narcotics involvement must be so risky and so expensive that it will lose its attractiveness. Possibly this could be ac-

2. Milton Halpern and Yong-Myun Rho, "Deaths from Narcoticism in New York City," in *The Int'l Journal of the Addictions,* Vol. 2, no. 1 (1967).

complished for the commercial operations, since they do, after all, operate according to market principles. It is patent, however, that risk of punishment has almost no impact on the essentially compulsive behavior of the drug user. In fact, the compulsion of the narcotic addict, the willingness to do anything to get the drug, forms a part of the definition of the addict. Yet, the hardline enforcement people, oblivious to the inconsistency, have unrelentingly urged severe sentences in order to deter the user as well as the seller.[3]

It would seem that in our hysteria and our irrational reaction to the controlling of drug abuse we have forced addicts into the life of crime, with the resultant long jail and prison terms. While New York State laws are not the most severe (Michigan and Ohio have that honor), they do the job of getting the narcotic addict out of circulation and into jail and prison. New York addicts spend a good part of their careers in jails and prison—nearly two-thirds (64%) of our sample said that they had been in jail or reform school at some time during their career, and another 17% had been arrested but had not served sentences.

As often happens in the white courts of America, in both the North and the South, blacks and Puerto Ricans more often served sentences after arrest than did whites. The same minority groups also served more time when they did go to jail. Nothing is more damning of the racist nature of our courts than this finding. When two youngsters, one white and the other black or Puerto Rican, go up in front of a judge for the same charges, the black or Puerto Rican one, in most cases, can figure on going to jail and staying there longer than the white.

Regardless of race, the older the addict is and the longer he uses heroin, the more likely he is to go to jail. No matter what precautions he takes, the odds are very high that he will eventually go to jail. Only 7% of those of our sample with long histories of heroin use (10 years or longer) had *never* been to jail or arrested.

It would seem that when an addict is arrested the first time he becomes involved in a system comprised of the police and the courts that causes him to begin a revolving door of arrest, detoxification, incarceration, release, readdiction, and so forth. Of all those (274) who said that they had been to jail or reform school at some time, half (53%) had been in jail four or more times and another quarter (26%) had been in two or three times. Arrest and incarceration become a not unexpected part of the career of the addict. There is a certain resignation among addicts to the ways in which society re-

3. William Butler Eldridge, *Narcotics and the Law* (New York: American Bar Foundation, distributed by New York University Press, 1962).

sponds to their actions. Characteristic of most groups who have found themselves cast out of the mainstream of society, they defend themselves against its assault on their lives by rejecting society and its values—this is the sub-culture of addiction.

I believe that there is a certain justification to this defense. The experience of jail and prisons is a devastating one; it leaves its mark on nearly everyone who experiences it. There is little in society to compare to the brutality and dehumanization that occur in prisons. Most of the prisons in America are places that serve only to control and punish offenders. Rehabilitation within most prisons is a sham; the hostility and defensiveness that most imprisonment causes acts against the meager rehabilitative efforts. Without resources and staff, prison administrations just go through the motions of establishing rehabilitation programs. Even the most dedicated and hardest fighting of prison administrators give in to society and its demand to control and punish the offender.

ARREST AND CONVICTION

Like beginning heroin use, the first arrests of those in our sample occurred early. Nearly half (49%) of the 422 had been arrested at least once by the time they were 18 years old, a quarter (24%) had been arrested by the time they were 16, and 8% were arrested before they were 13 years old. If this is not bad enough, there is now a trend toward earlier arrests among those recently addicted, with older, long-term users (10 years or more) arrested much later in life than younger, short-term users. Currently, young drug users are apprehended earlier than their older counterparts. This is undoubtedly due to the closer surveillance of the expanded narcotics police in New York.

One of the continuing and often tedious arguments between writers and researchers in the field is the debate over whether an addict is criminal before addiction or not. Opposing sides in the argument were crystallized by Alfred Lindesmith, one of the pioneer sociologists in the field, and Henry Anslinger, the former Chief of the Federal Narcotic Bureau. Lindesmith's position was that the addict is not criminal before addiction and only becomes criminal as a consequence of his addiction. He stated that the crimes of drug users were most often crimes against property and were committed only to acquire money to get drugs. Furthermore, he contended that as heroin is a depressant, it did not directly influence persons to commit crimes. Rather, given a regular supply of heroin, the physical action of the drug would probably inhibit criminal actions.

Anslinger, at the other extreme, argues that drug abuse and addiction are consequences of criminal activity or associations. The addict is either a criminal or well on the road to becoming a criminal before his drug abuse and addiction begin. After addiction he simply has another reason for continuing a career of crime.

In an effort to clarify this argument we asked everyone in our sample if he had been arrested before he had started using heroin. Roughly half (47%) reported that they *had* been arrested before using heroin and half (53%) said they had *not* (the differences are not statistically significant). This finding supports neither Lindesmith nor Anslinger—some were arrested and some were not.

Seen in relation to other data gathered on arrest before addiction, it would appear that historically the majority of addicts were *not* arrested until after their addiction, but that in recent years there is a trend for more to have been arrested before. Whatever the outcome of this tired old saw of an argument, the addict in our society is defined as a criminal and treated as such. Possession of heroin is illegal and as long as it is defined as such the addict will be treated as a criminal.

Unlike many cities in America (Los Angeles in particular), law enforcement in New York City is much less focused upon the user than upon the seller of the drugs. Addicts are omnipresent in New York; they appear to be all over the city. Several pan-handled money regularly along Broadway at 115th Street near the office of our study. Two blocks from the neighborhood I lived in in Brooklyn (Cobble Hill) there was a regular congregation of addicts. They seem in some respects to permeate all of the life of New York.

Indeed, if the police wanted to they could fill the jails of New York with users. But the police regularly proclaim that their concern is not with misdemeanor arrests (for possession) but with felonies. The theory is that if they arrest the seller they will be more able to control the problem. Unfortunately this proclamation is transformed into action not against the importers or kilo connections but against the addict sellers—ounce dealers and street pushers. These are the most common and easiest to detect.

During the first months of the study one of our best research assistants, Tom Fortuin, made preliminary field visits to several members of the City and Federal Bureaus of Narcotics in preparation for a more detailed study of police operations we planned to make. Unfortunately, the detailed study was not made because we weren't always as tactful as we might have been with the Federal Bureau of Narcotics, but we did learn something of the operations of the city police.

According to official policy police investigation in New York City occurs at two levels among the four levels of sales that we outlined earlier. The Federal Bureau of Narcotics and the Special Investigation Unit of New York City's Narcotics Bureau concentrate most of their efforts and activity on the larger operators—importers, kilo connections, and larger wholesale sellers like Watusi and Goldfinger, who are described here by a plainclothes detective:

> Yes, a couple of the two biggest wholesalers are Watusi and Goldfinger. They're so big they don't get anywhere near the street; they probably don't even touch or see heroin. They got big factories, they have girls and women to bag the stuff, paying as much as $100 a day to do this. Goldfinger marks his bags with a tape. It's like walking into a supermarket with name brands. Another one marks his bags with a gold star. Then we got "007" too; he's recent with the James Bond movies. All of these men are known to the police, but its another matter to arrest them. These fellows have friends and good lawyers; they are usually out of jail in a matter of hours. It's difficult to get anything to stick with these fellows.

The ounce dealers, street sellers, and users get the attention of area squads of the City Narcotics Bureau, plainclothes detectives, and police officers of the local precincts. These levels of sellers are, usually to a man, addicts who operate on a relatively small margin of profit and take the largest risks, in that they are often exposed to police surveillance. Most of the arrests made by the City Narcotics Squad in any given day, week, or month are at this level because the addict-sellers are the most numerous. Although we were never able to determine the exact allocation of staff and monies of the City's Narcotics Bureau, it was our impression that most of the effort of the Narcotics Bureau was at this level.

Arrests made by police and plainclothes detectives at the precinct level usually result from an investigation of other crimes. An addict is apprehended for a theft or a burglary and when he is searched narcotics are discovered, so he is charged with possession. Roughly half of the drug arrests are made in this way.

The narcotics squads state that they are not concerned with the user (who in most instances would be charged with misdemeanor possession) but only with felonies—possession of an ounce or more of narcotics, possession with intent to sell, and sales. Sales, it is said, are their main concern—as a plainclothes detective explained:

The overwhelming majority of arrests made by narcotics squads are made after sale to one of the squad's agents. Usually, two attempts to buy drugs by the agent are made before the suspect is arrested and charged. We usually have a cover detective who watches the transaction, follows the seller, and arrests him at a later date. This is done usually a couple of weeks later to preserve the cover of the agent. In this way when the suspect is picked up he knows that he has been selling but usually does not know which of the sales he made to an undercover agent. The result is often an early plea of guilty. Since the process usually produces iron-clad evidence there is little problem getting complaints signed by the D.A.'s office and fewer problems with the courts.

The principal sources of information are informers and the plainclothesman's own observations on the street. Addicts are often willing informants, as is vouched by one plainclothesman:

> If you arrest somebody strung out—going through withdrawal—it's no difficulty getting him to turn informant. If the addict is bad enough off, he'll do anything for his drugs. This works to our advantage, too.
>
> Sometimes they'll tell you about pushers, hoping to get a lesser charge. You bust 'em on a felony possession and they try anything to get it busted to a misdemeanor. Some of these guys would tell on their mother if they thought they could get something for it. . . .
>
> Hard criminal types—that's something else; they wouldn't tell you anything. There aren't so many of them though. . . .
>
> Once in a while somebody who has been burnt by a seller will tell you all about him. They do it to get even. This doesn't happen all that much, though.

When no other information is available the agents will cruise areas of high drug activity and approach suspects as they find them, harass cars in the area from upstate or with out-of-state license plates, and pose as addicts themselves. Occasionally they establish observation posts on rooftops to observe buying and selling on the street. A good deal of selling in New York is conducted on the street because the pusher is afraid that addicts will take him off if he moves off the street into hallways or apartments. Now and then TV cameras are used to film sales in areas of dense activity. One detective described it for us:

> Last winter we set up TV cameras in vacant apartments and filmed several sales on 116th Street. We posed as plumbers, brought the equipment into the apartment, and had it going for a couple of days. You couldn't believe all the action there; the squad might have collared at least 16,000 [an overestimate] last year alone. The street was so thick that you could make an arrest on one end, come back a couple of hours later, and make another arrest at the other end.

There were so many users and sellers then that a single arrest wouldn't heat up the area at all. We cleaned it out, but the action just moved down to 115th Street.

Little if any information is garnered from citizens' complaints, even though addiction and sales of drugs are among the most frequent complaints made by citizens of New York. Generally this kind of information is too general, and the District Attorney's and the courts' requirement of good evidence prevents police from making mass sweeps of known users or sellers.

By way of illustrating the rather improvised and haphazard methods of the narcotics squad, I've included portions of a long field report by our research assistant, Tom Fortuin, who traveled with the squad in Central Harlem:

Three of us got into Evans'* blue, two-door, five year old Ford and followed Smith as he parked his car. Afterwards we looked for a bank to cash paychecks. . . . On the way to the bank at the corner of 5th Avenue and 135th Street, Smith spotted a tall, thin, black man dressed in an old raincoat and hat, smoking a long cigarette. This was an informant; Smith got out of the car and arranged to meet the informant at 113th Street and Lenox Avenue in an hour.

After stopping at that bank we then toured areas known to be sites of many drug sales. We drove up and down Lenox Avenue at about 127th Street. We saw several standing crowds which we found to be crap games. We stopped at every light, red or green, while the plain-clothesmen observed front and back. Any sign of an exchange of money and closed fists was regarded as suspicious.

At one corner Smith called my attention to a man's hands; they were large and puffy [often an indication of addiction or repeated injections in the hands]. The man walked down the street and went into a restaurant. He looked clean and well-dressed in a long tan raincoat. As he emerged from the restaurant, he spotted us, took something from his hands and put it into the breast pocket of his shirt.

We followed him a short distance down the street, then Smith and Holmes got out of the car. All the while the man never looked back at the car, which Evans interpreted as a suspicious sign. Holmes and Smith ran up behind the man, reaching him as he got to the curb to cross the street. One on each side they took him into a nearby housing project while Evans and I waited in the car.

After they returned, Holmes joked that he had to warn the suspect not to cut Hugh Smith. The man had been clean (they searched him), but was carrying a large knife in his raincoat pocket. The opened blade was rolled into a handkerchief like a sheath; it was ready for use. Holmes returned the man's blade to him after the search and all three emerged from the housing project; the suspect looking indignant.

* All names in the report have been changed.

We were now on our way to meet the informant seen earlier. Crossing Lenox Avenue we saw a man with a large roll of bills get into a brand new, shiny brown Oldsmobile. Evans identified him as the "digitarian, the policy man." As we approached he looked back at us and immediately went about his business in a very official manner. Smith said, "Isn't it amazing how they can spot us just the way we can spot them." As we pulled up next to the Oldsmobile at the traffic light, the "digitarian" was aware of us but refused to look in our direction. Holmes rolled down the window and caught the man's attention. "Getting sick of Cadillacs?" he asked the policy man, laughed, and moved on.

As we arrived at 113th Street and Lenox, the informant was just arriving. We pulled up to the curb and Smith got out and entered a nearby building. The informant followed him in. Shortly thereafter they both exited, Smith first and the informant a few minutes later. He reported that the man had stopped on 115th Street a few minutes before coming to 113th Street to see who was selling on the street and then described two men who were. All three went over the descriptions of the men.

We then proceeded to 115th Street. On the way they spotted a recent model, blue-green metallic-colored Tempest with a New York license plate. Three young, white youths were inside with an older black man about 35 years old in the back. The detectives speculated that this group was from Westchester and had come down to cop. Holmes observed that the driver was drinking a soda, which he interpreted as a sure sign he was a heroin user. "If we didn't have this lead, we'd follow that car," someone explained.

We drove around a few more minutes to give the informant time to get back to 115th Street. Holmes joked about one informant who tried to help identify sellers, "He would move up next to a pusher and make signs to us. He put on his sun glasses or took off his coat. That stupid bastard might just as well send off flares."

A few minutes later we stopped at Lenox and 115th Street. Evans and Smith got out this time. They returned in a short while and said that the sellers had left the street.

At one point on the street Smith said that the informant had turned and spoken to Smith, who was behind him. Holmes thought this was a dangerous and stupid thing to do. I asked what would happen if the sellers knew of the informant's activities. "He's dead," Evans responded. "Just the other week, a man was pushed off the roof of a tenement and killed. He wasn't cool enough."

Continuing about informants, I asked how much an informant might receive. "If he gives us good information and we make an arrest, we'll give him $5 or $10. We only have $40 a month and gas money to spend on this kind of thing. . . ."

A few minutes later we met the informant again on 113th Street and then we went back to 115th. They observed two men who appeared to be working together that fit the description given by the informant. They suspected that one with a felt fedora was handling the money and the second one the drugs. We parked down the street about 3/4 of a block away; all three alighted. They came back a half an hour later and described what happened. "Smith spotted the hatted dude with a bag in his hand. He put his arm around him in a firm arm lock, but the man began to struggle and they both fell to the curb. By the time Evans and I got there the dude had dropped the shit and kicked it away. A junkie who was looking on said some kid picked it up and ran upstairs. We searched the handler, found nothing, and let him go."

The men were disappointed that they had missed the possible arrest. We proceeded to 110th Street where we again met the informant. Holmes got out and talked to him; he came back and said that the informant wanted cigarette money. He got cigarettes out of the back of the car and went to the informant again. When he returned he said he had given the informant a quarter for soup.

Then we returned to 115th Street from the East this time. As we entered the street, someone hollered "Police!" There were several groups on the street—all said to be addicts. We drove to the end of the street and Smith went into a barbershop. The barber told him that the younger kids were planning to throw bottles down from the roof if we came through there again.

Back in the car we drove again. Holmes explained why they were disappointed that the tip from the informant hadn't paid off, "If you know who you're looking for, that's half the battle. Without an informant you have to go to the roofs to watch for sales. Sometimes you have to use binoculars not to be seen yourself."

As we drove by a supermarket Smith sighted a group of three teenagers walking along that he thought looked suspicious. Smith jumped out and followed the boys through the supermarket. We drove around the block to the back door and watched the boys emerge in a few minutes. Smith came out a minute behind them and indicated by gestures that they should follow the boy wearing a hat. The boys entered a candy and record shop; the three detectives followed them in. Inside they searched the tall one with the hat and found nothing. They came out talking with the boys.

We continued to tour around, stopping at an address where drugs were known to have been sold. A woman in the window immediately spotted us. A boy on the street casually strolled by and said, "Hello, Officer." No one laughed. Holmes got out again but came back shortly, shaking his head.

We proceeded to Fifth Avenue and Smith went into a bar to make a phone call to Lt. Harris. Lt. Smith wanted him to telephone a detective who worked outside the city who had previously worked narcotics about a possible tip. The detective had been out when he called.

We proceeded to 126th Street and parked behind the Apollo Theater. All three alighted and Evans returned in about five minutes and explained that they had made an arrest. At 8th Avenue and 126th Street a man had approached Holmes and offered to sell him blue jackets ($5 caps of cocaine) at $5 a cap. Evans and I drove up 126th Street to the end of the street where the man was being held so that he could be gotten into the car without "heating up" the neighborhood.

The apprehended seller got into the back seat and sat between Smith and me, his hand-cuffed hands in his lap. He was clean and well-dressed in patterned woolen pants with blue and red stripes and a short stylish raincoat. Once in the car the mood was more jovial than before. All of a sudden everyone had a story to tell.

The suspect was less happy and asked, "Do you have to bring me in?"

Holmes replied, "Have to bring you in? Why the way you were selling out there you should have had a license. Have you ever been arrested before?"

"Yes," he replied quietly, looking into his lap.

The conversation between the three detectives was fast and funny. They were pleased with their achievement.

Back at the 28th Precinct, we all went up to the second floor to the detention cell and to fill out the arrest forms. The charge was intent to sell rather than sales because Smith had made the arrest before the money had exchanged hands. Holmes explained that there were no witnesses and it would be simpler to claim that the money had actually touched the defendant's hands. "But the D.A. won't believe it. He won't believe us anyway."

Smith and Evans returned to 126th Street to see if they could make another arrest. Holmes was filling out the forms and talked to the suspect rather jovially, but kindly. He was proud of the fact that he had been mistaken for a junkie. "I look like a junkie, thin and all. You thought you'd seen me—you'd seen me before." The accused nodded yes; he was being as cooperative and agreeable as possible.

Holmes filled out all the necessary forms. Although he was clowning around a bit, I could see his hands shake a bit as he rested them on the typewriter; the excitement of the chase had not yet worn off.

A half an hour later, Evans came back with a man and a woman and said they had another arrest. The two had been acting as a team; the woman was carrying clothes on a hanger over her arm. Heroin was in the pockets of the garments. . . . The write-up was long and laborious. I left them at 6:00 p.m.; they said they were going to work into the night and try to get a couple more arrests.

Unfortunately, we were unable to make any extensive observation of the methods of the narcotics squad, but discussions with a number of addicts with more than a little experience of police methods, albeit from the receiving end, confirm our observation.

Arrest does not always result in conviction; not by any means does every addict "cop" a guilty plea. The proportion of arrests to convictions on drug charges for our sample was 2:1—two arrests for every conviction. For charges other than drugs, it was 3:1. Surpris-

ingly there was a fairly large number who had never been arrested
on drug charges (more than a third, 37%), and even larger numbers
had never been convicted (72%). Many of these, however, were beginning users or persons only in danger of being addicted.

Certainly some of the arrests made are illegal—many users described to our interviewers instances of illegal entry, of planting
drugs, and so forth—but they occur much less often than one would
expect. New York courts are quite zealous about evidence require-
ments. Perhaps New York judges are less startled by drug arrests,
seeing so many, or have more knowledge of police methods than in
other states. Both the Courts and the District Attorney require good
evidence that will withstand scrutiny.

Surprisingly, the attitudes of the narcotics squad were not as
vindictive or scornful of heroin users as one would think. A good
number expressed the attitude that addicts were sick and needed
medical help. One even advocated the legalization of heroin.

POLICE ACTIVITIES

A great many police activities in New York are concerned with
the enforcement of narcotic laws and involve heroin. During the
first year of the study, 1968, New York police made 22,428 narcotics
arrests. More than two out of every five (43%) were felonies, and
three out of every four (75%) involved heroin.

Drug arrests have increased sharply in New York since 1964,
when the staff of the Narcotics Bureau was increased substantially.
Prior to 1964 the yearly increases were steady (excepting 1961), but
not dramatic. Since 1963 there have been steady increases, with
dramatic increases in 1964 (57%), 1966 (18%), and 1968 (28%). This
trend continued in 1969, with more than 35,000 arrests made—an
increase of 57% over 1968. These general trends were summarized
by George Nash and Eli Cohen, in an analysis of narcotic arrests for
the 10-year period 1957–1967:

> What is striking, along with the increase in the number of narcotics
> arrests, is the total number. At the rate of arrests occurring in 1967,
> approximately 49 persons were arrested in New York City every day
> of the year (during 1969 this number increased to 96 each day). Nar-
> cotic felony arrests amounted to 9.3% of all felony arrests in 1966
> and were the fifth highest category after felonious assault, burglary,
> larceny of a motor vehicle, and robbery. Narcotic misdemeanor ar-
> rests accounted for 7.5% of all misdemeanors, but were the second
> highest category behind violation of motor vehicle laws. Overall,

narcotic arrests in N.Y.C. in 1966 account for 8% of all arrests for felonies and misdemeanors. It is interesting to note that while narcotic arrests have been rising, non-narcotic arrests in New York City have been decreasing since 1962, and total arrests have been decreasing since 1964.[4]

Despite these police activities there is a steady flow of heroin into New York City, which prompted Chief Counsel Joseph Fisch of the New York State Commission of Investigation to judge after investigation in 1971 that the New York Police Department's efforts were ". . . a failure, a monumental waste of manpower and money" that had had "no appreciable effect on the flow of drugs in New York City. . . ." Continuing, Mr. Fisch cited police corruption, poorly trained and inadequately supervised detectives, and a quota system for felony arrests that forced detectives to focus efforts on low-level dealers and pushers rather than on the time-consuming and complicated arrests of importers and connections.[5]

During the Commission's investigation several former policemen testified about their own involvement in narcotics traffic—selling heroin and receiving payoffs. Payoffs are said to be so prevalent among narcotics detectives as to cause the City Department's own corruption experts, Inspectors Joseph McGovern and Donald F. Cowley, to cite narcotics as the largest single source of graft in the police department, even over gambling, which had for years been the major source. Police efforts hampered by corruption of this magnitude must have but little, if any, control over drug traffic.

Much police effort to arrest low-level heroin dealers and pushers is fruitless. As we saw in the previous chapter, most addicts (82%) sell drugs at some time in their careers; lower-level drug sellers and users are in most cases one and the same. This, I believe, should be given consideration when legislators enact laws that attempt to differentiate between seller and user and when police departments—as a matter of policy—concentrate their efforts on drug sellers.

In recent years, in the belief that it was not the user but the seller who was the "bad guy," the menace in drug transactions, police have pushed for and legislators have enacted harsher and harsher sentences for drug sales. The hope has been to control drug sales and lessen the number of users by concentrating on the nefarious seller. This would, perhaps be a reasonable tactic if police efforts

4. George Nash and Eli Cohen, "An Analysis of New York City Police Statistics for Narcotic Arrests During the Period 1957–1967" (Mimeographed, Columbia University Bureau of Applied Social Research, March 1969).
    5. Articles in *The New York Times* on April 21 and 25 and May 2, 1971, and *The Village Voice*, April 22, 1971.

were concentrated on traffickers and connections and if they were effective in finding and arresting them, but this is not the case in New York. New York narcotics police do *not* concentrate on the large transactions of connections and traffickers but upon the more numerous pushers and dealers. In most instances New York Narcotics police have arrest quotas; in order to satisfy these, individual officers must forego the long and tedious investigations necessary for the apprehension of large sellers. As pushers and dealers are easier to detect and more numerous, the police naturally gravitate towards them to fill their quotas of felony arrests. Within this system, the individual officer gets his quota and the police department gets large impressive statistics, but there is little effect upon drug sales or abuse, because for every street pusher or dealer the police arrest, there is another addict to take his place. Some addicts may shy away from the risks of drug sales, but most are quite willing to sell drugs; it is most certainly the easiest way to support a drug habit.

Harsher and harsher prison sentences for drug sales do little more than assure society that addicts will go to jail for longer terms. This is not the way to control drug distribution. It would be much easier to control it by deflating the black-market price of heroin so that the profits for importation and large sales would not be worth the risks of arrest. There is currently a good deal of money available in large heroin transactions and there will always be those who will risk arrest to make big money. Take away the possibility of that big money, and there will be fewer persons involved in the black market.

But this would be a rational way to deal with "the problem" and I have long since given up the thought that we will ever deal with addiction rationally. Any review of the history of addiction in the United States will show that as a country we have always responded in the most irrational ways towards addicts. Perhaps if fifty years ago we had let doctors treat addicts as the British did instead of abdicating the responsibility to the Federal Bureau of Narcotics we would not have the large numbers of addicts we do.

Contrary to Dr. Henry Brill's criticism[6] and to some newspaper reports, the "British system"—that allows doctors rather than police to treat addicts—has *not* failed. There were abuses in the earlier British approach, which let any doctor prescribe for an addict, that resulted in a small number of doctors over-prescribing drugs—with the excess sold by addicts. But England, like the United States since the 1950s, has experienced an upsurge in the interest

6. Henry Brill and Granville W. Larimore, "Second on-Site Study of the British Narcotic System," in *N.A.C.C. Reprints*, Vol. 1, no. 2 (1968).

and use of all drugs, legal and illegal, so there was bound to be an increase in the number of addicts. The British Home Office could see from their records the seriousness of the increase in the numbers of known addicts: from 470 in 1961 to 1,729 in 1967.[7] As a consequence, the methods of treating addicts were reorganized into the present system. In 1968 drug treatment centers were established, and it is only in these centers that an addict may be maintained on heroin or any other drug. Controls have been firmly established over the prescription of drugs, but doctors still treat addicts and they are not considered criminals.

Shortly after the clinics opened in 1968 there was a sizable increase in the numbers of addicts known to the Home Office, an increase to 2,782. This happened for two reasons: the new law required that *all* addicts be reported to the Home Office, and everyone *had* to go to a treatment center to get his needed drugs. In 1969 the numbers of new addicts entering treatment centers declined dramatically, and there were only 99 addicts added to the lists of those already known. Since then the number of new cases has been decreasing every month. It is also expected that with the growth of abstention programs and the beginning use of oral methadone maintenance programs, the number of heroin users at these clinics will begin to decline.

This method—treating addiction as a medical rather than criminal problem—has not failed.[8] The number of addicts did increase, but this may be attributed to abuses by individual doctors and to a general upsurge in interest in all psychoactive drugs, legal and illegal and in the incidence of all users. I lived in England during part of this period of increase (1963–1966), and there was, as in the United States, an upsurge in the use and abuse of LSD, amphetamines, and barbiturates, particularly among the young. This increased interest and use may account for much of the increase in the number of addicts. Perhaps if our methods of recording addicts had been better (there was nothing like New York City's Narcotic Registry then) we would have recognized an increase similar to that in England, as there are most definitely similarities in the increasing drug cultures of both countries.

7. D. V. Hawks, "The Dimensions of Drug Dependence in the United Kingdom," in *The International Journal of the Addictions*, Vol. 6, no. 1 (1971).
8. For a current description, see Edgar May, "Drugs Without Crime: A Report on the British Success with Heroin Addiction," in *Harper's Magazine*, July 1971.

Going to
Treatment

A SHORT HISTORY OF MAJOR
TREATMENT EFFORTS

Only since World War II has any organized treatment—medical, psychiatric, and self-help—begun to figure, like arrest and incarceration, in the overall careers of addicts. Before that, medical treatment (except in federal hospitals) was almost forbidden the addict. First the Harrison Act of 1914, which required that addicts obtain narcotics from doctors registered under the act and that such transactions be recorded, then a Supreme Court decision (*U.S. vs Jin Fuey Moy*), which ruled that possession of smuggled drugs was a violation of the law, and then several subsequent decisions against doctors (*U.S. vs Webb 1919, U.S. vs Jin Fuey Moy 1920, and U.S. vs Behrman 1920 and 1922*), which discouraged doctors from legally prescribing drugs either to maintain or to detoxify addicts outside of a hospital, all acted to define addiction in an oblique way as criminal and literally to forbid the addict medical treatment.

Surprisingly, the first medical treatment of addicts in organized, ambulatory clinics was started at the instigation of the Internal Revenue Service, the original enforcers of the Harrison Act. In 1919 forty-four clinics were established in nearly as many cities and states to provide short-term, emergency treatment for addicts in an attempt to deter the rising number of illegal sales. This treatment consisted of withdrawal, temporary maintenance (in some cases), and "cure."

All of these clinics were short-lived; the clinic in Shreveport, Louisiana, was open the longest—four years. In a sudden reversal of policy, a federal edict forced them all to close when agents of the Prohibition Unit of the Internal Revenue Service claimed that all the clinics were over-prescribing drugs and that they were being operated inefficiently. Some clinics may have been badly run but not all of them, and certainly not the Shreveport clinic, which, from a letter written by the then Commissioner of the Shreveport Department of Public Safety, seems to have been both efficient and in control of its prescription practices:

> . . . I wish to say that from a police standpoint, the City of Shreveport is greatly benefited by [the clinic] being here. It has practically eliminated the bootlegger who deals in narcotics, and in this way alone has reduced the number of possible future dope users. . . .
>
> Before the establishment of the Clinic a great number of criminals prosecuted through this department were those addicted with the use of opiates. Now, however, it is very seldom that we have to prosecute this class, and we are able to keep a direct line upon anyone who might sell morphine, cocaine and such other drugs as are prohibited by law. . . .
>
> Our records show that the Clinic here has cured a number of those afflicted with this habit, and some are working here and are citizens that respect themselves and are respected by this department. The authorities in charge of the Police Department in Shreveport would regard it a calamity should this Clinic be removed from this point, and we are as earnestly for it at the present time as we were bitterly opposed to it upon its institution here. We cannot speak in too high terms of Dr. Butler [Director of the Clinic] and his methods used at the dispensary.[1]

But it, too, like the rest, fell in 1923 under the pressure from the Internal Revenue Service.

At about the same time that these clinics were started and then stopped, the Supreme Court discouraged doctors from providing medical treatment to addicts in private practice outside of established hospitals. These are the Webb, Jin Fuey Moy, and Behrman decisions, with their implicit assumption that addiction was not a medical condition that required medical treatment, but a willful vice or indulgence that should be subject to punishment.

Under conditions of the law and within the limits of court decisions, hospitals could have offered some treatment to addicts, but

1. Letter from the Commissioner of the Shreveport Department of Public Safety to the President of the Louisiana State Board of Health, 1920.

they, like private doctors, had been intimidated by the government and completely shunned the addict. They also thought that addiction was a vice or social problem rather than a treatable medical condition.

Only years later was any concerted effort made to view addiction as a treatable condition. In 1929 Congress authorized the establishment of two Public Health Service hospitals to treat addicts who volunteered or who had committed offenses against Federal narcotics laws. These hospitals were located at Lexington, Kentucky, and Ft. Worth, Texas; the first was opened in 1935 and is still operating, the second was opened in 1938 and closed in 1971.

Both hospitals were, until recently, little more than glorified prisons with doctors and researchers in attendance despite their hospital designations. Dr. Marie Nyswander has described her stay in Lexington during World War II:

> The year I spent at Lexington . . . was the most miserable I'd ever known. Because of the way I'd been raised, I was totally unequipped to cope with the attitudes which prevail in a prison, and that is essentially what Lexington is. I'd never had anything to do with addicts before and when I left I never wanted to see another one as long as I lived.[2]

Fortunately for the many addicts Dr. Nyswander has subsequently treated at the East Harlem Protestant Parish and at the Methadone Maintenance Program at the Morris Bernstein Institute, she changed her mind and has dedicated her very productive life to finding more humane and effective ways to treat addicts.

Alexander King, a former nighttime TV talk-show interviewer, writer, and painter who was addicted medically and went to Lexington three different times, gives us the addict's view of that hospital:

> It was not exactly a country club; it was and is, predominantly a federal prison, with certain hospital overtones. For some unimaginable appeasement of purely verbal protocol, all the prisoners, including the ones who are serving fifteen years, are called "patients" by the staff. The staff is called "Hacks" and "Croakers" by the patients. The croakers are the doctors.
>
> Let me say at once that I found no individual villains among the people who were employed there. The real blame of the place lies in its undefined character and status.
>
> In ordinary prisons there are certain established routines which penologists have found empirically workable. [sic] In hospitals the

2. Nat Hentoff, *A Doctor among the Addicts* (New York: Grove Press, Inc., 1970).

patients might be considered nuisances (by the working staff), but
they are not considered criminals. Well in Lexington you are both.
I've thought a good deal about it and it is nobody's fault. It is one
of those unsolveable problems that modern life has puked up, and I
haven't many important suggestions for improvement.[3]

King did, however, abstain from opiates after one of these stays at
Lexington, and his book suggests that he met a sympathetic doctor
there who gave him some help and understanding. He did not, however, attribute his abstention to Lexington.

As one would expect, the prison-like treatment at Lexington,
which usually consisted of detoxification, help with education, and
psychotherapy in group and private sessions, was never very effective
with urban addicts. There have been several evaluations made of
Lexington's urban addict patients from follow-ups as short as one
year and as long as ten years after release. These evaluations show
that most addicts relapse to drugs shortly after they leave the hospital; the percentages range from 80% to 99%.

Two long-range follow-ups, of five and ten years, have found
that although the addicts had relapsed after leaving the hospital,
many were drug free at the time of contact; 40% in the five-year
study[4] and 47% in the ten-year study.[5] Lexington Hospital and its
apologists[6] assume credit for these abstentions, but so much inter-
vened in the lives of the ex-patients (other treatment, arrest and
incarceration, maturation, and so forth) that it is impossible to
attribute the abstention to any one factor and particularly difficult
to attribute it to a hospitalization that occurred so long before the
time of contact.

The next major movement to attempt to treat addicts arose
among the addicts themselves. This was Synanon and the numerous
other self-help communities that sprang up out of the original idea.
Charles Dederich, something of a godlike, gruff, father figure, started
Synanon with a small group of addicts in Ocean Park, California, in
1958, modeling it loosely after Alcoholics Anonymous. Adapting

    3. Alexander King, *Mine Enemy Grows Older* (New York: Simon & Shuster,
Inc., 1958).
    4. Henrietta Duval, Ben Locke, and Leon Brill, "Follow-up Study of Nar-
cotic Addicts Five Years after Hospitalization," in *Public Health Reports,* Vol.
98, no. 3 (1963).
    5. George Vaillant, "A Twelve-Year Follow-up of New York Narcotic
Addicts: I. The Relation of Treatment to Outcome," in *The American Journal
of Psychiatry,* Vol. 122, no. 7 (1966).
    6. One of the most recent apologists of Lexington is Frederick B. Glaser,
"Misinformation about Drugs: A Problem for Drug Abuse Education," in *The
International Journal of the Addictions,* Vol. 5, no. 1 (1970).

group-therapy techniques and using the social controls of a community in a novel way, Synanon changed the behavior of addicts and created the first visible group of ex-addicts. Both the visibility and the self-help ideas of Synanon challenged existing treatment methods, and Synanon "splitees" (strangely enough Synanon considers all splitees dead—meaning they are using drugs—disdaining the idea that anyone would ever think of leaving Synanon) have developed similar therapeutic communities all over the country and particularly in New York.[7]

Currently Synanon is a thriving way of life. They now own and operate their own businesses, own considerable land in California, have their own experimental schools, and are creating a new town for their residents. The present population of Synanon encompasses a much broader group than addicts. The program attracts alcoholics, persons with various mental-health and social problems, and a certain number of "normals" who come to Synanon for its relevant and active community life.

The essential appeal of Synanon is to middle-class whites who are discontented with their lives and with society and are willing to give themselves up to the idea of Synanon and the "higher" goals of the community. It does not now reach (and has not in the past) many of the working-class black or Spanish-speaking addicts who constitute most of California's addict population.

There have been no formal evaluations of Synanon and it is not likely that there will be any. They are, generally, distrustful of research and researchers, perhaps with some justifications. Like blacks, addicts have been over-researched, and many researchers can be condescending and insensitive.

Early in 1950 newspapers in New York City had a series of articles about a seeming increase in the numbers of teenage addicts in the city. At that time there was no central registry of known addicts in New York so it is not known whether this supposed increase was real or not. However, as a result of this campaign the City Department of Hospitals opened Riverside Hospital to treat adolescent addicts.

Treatment was initiated with a large staff of psychiatrists, psychologists, social workers, teachers, occupational therapists, recrea-

7. There are three good descriptions of Synanon: Lewis Yablonsky, *Synanon, The Tunnel Back* (New York: The Macmillan Company, 1967); Rita Volkman and Donald R. Cressey, "Differential Association and Rehabilitation of Drug Addicts," in *American Journal of Sociology,* Vol. 69 (1963); and Daniel Casriel, *So Fair a House: The Story of Synanon* (Englewood Cliffs, N.J.: Prentice-Hall, Inc., 1963).

tional therapists, and guards in a 141-bed hospital. It followed the Lexington model for the most part, but with much less emphasis on security.

This hospital opened in 1955 with both the city and state sharing the costs of the program. In 1957 the state contracted with the Columbia University School of Public Health to make an evaluation of the effectiveness of the program. Dr. Ray Trussell, Harold Alkne, and Sherman Patrick undertook a follow-up of 247 adolescents who had entered the hospital in 1955. Recently, Dr. Trussell summarized anew their findings at the Second National Methadone Maintenance Conference:

> It turned out that the best way to find these people was to keep an eye on hospital admissions and admissions to penal institutions. Of all the interviews that were held, only 14% were held outside of a hospital or a jail. Briefly, the data collected in this study indicated that by 1958, among the 247, there had been 11 deaths, a very high death rate for this age group. . . .
>
> What was most startling was the fact that of the entire group, only eight had never returned to the use of drugs and those eight to a man swore that they had never been addicted. They had been caught in possession, they had been committed, they had put in their time and gone home, and that was the end of the episode as far as they were concerned.
>
> So the city was operating a closed community with all the various professional disciplines at work with a success rate of zero [actually 91% relapsed to daily heroin use] for all the patients admitted in 1955.[8]

Despite this obviously negative evaluation Riverside Hospital continued to operate until 1961 and was only closed then because Dr. Trussell closed it himself when he became Commissioner of Hospitals under Mayor Wagner. Addiction in New York had become a political issue and the city would not close the hospital even when they knew it was ineffective. This experience should be a lesson to all of those who start drug treatment programs. Independent evaluation should be the order for every program—few people are able to be objective about their own houses—and programs must act on these evaluations or, out of bureaucratic inertia and political expediency, public funds will be spent on expensive programs long after they are proven to have little or no effectiveness. This, as we will see later, is the case with California's Rehabilitation Center and,

8. Ray E. Trussell, "Treatment of Narcotic Addicts in New York City," in *The International Journal of the Addictions*, Vol. 5, no. 3 (1970).

perhaps, New York State's Narcotic Addiction Control Commission's abstention programs.

Despite the obvious failure of Riverside Hospital, the hospital model of treatment was instituted once again by the New York State Department of Mental Hygiene in state mental hospitals. In 1959 Manhattan State Hospital, located on Wards Island in New York City, established a narcotics treatment unit that is still operating today. This treatment unit was a precursor of the 1960 changes in the mental hygiene laws that allowed the state to commit addicts voluntarily to mental hospitals for treatment. This was the beginning of the idea of civil commitment of narcotic addicts in New York and culminated in the present laws and the vast program that I will write about later.

Under revision of this law in 1962 drug treatment units were established in seven more state mental hospitals, with separate aftercare units to serve those leaving the hospitals. Treatment after detoxification usually consisted of group and individual therapy, with educational and vocational training in separate closed drug units. There was little emphasis placed on security, and many persons simply walked out of the units, came back after they were picked up on a warrant, and walked off again, and so forth.

There was no formal or published evaluation made of the mental hygiene program, but there was a good deal of criticism of the program in the newspapers and, by 1966, a general feeling among legislators that like its predecessors, Lexington and Riverside Hospitals, the program had failed in its efforts to treat and rehabilitate addicts. All but one of the units, Manhattan State Hospital, were closed in 1968 after the Narcotic Addiction Control Commission took over the responsibility for civil and criminal commitments.

THE USE OF TREATMENT FACILITIES

All of the men in our samples were in treatment at the time of the interviews. For nearly half, this was one of at least two stays in some treatment facility; 48% reported that they had stayed at least overnight in some narcotic treatment center. For many this was part of a recurring pattern of use; more than one out of every five (22%) said that they had been in treatment three or more times previously, while the remaining 26% reported that they had been in one or two times before their current stay.

More than 25 different treatment facilities were cited by the samples. Those cited the most often were two detoxification centers, Morris Bernstein Institute and Metropolitan Hospital. Detoxification is the first step in any abstention program and while it is formally a treatment, in the medical sense, it is *not*, for the most part, used as such by addicts. The addict uses detoxification more as a service or refuge than as a formal treatment.

Whenever an addict's tolerance develops to such an extent that he finds it difficult to get high or even maintain himself without suffering recurrent or prolonged withdrawal sickness, he will attempt some withdrawal. This is often done on the streets by the addict himself, with the aid of dolphines, barbiturates, or tranquilizers. With a supply of dollies the addict can gradually reduce his tolerance for heroin to a manageable dosage, one that he can afford and that will allow him to get high.

When a detoxification facility is available and he can get into it within a reasonable time he will use it. The needs to reduce tolerances and to ease various pressures from society—to clean up for a court appearance after an arrest, to appease a parole or probation officer's demands to clean up, to obviate pressures exerted by his family—are the principle reasons why addicts go to detoxification facilities. It is very seldom that an addict goes to detoxification because he wants to give up the use of heroin.

Morris Bernstein Institute, Metropolitan Hospital, and Interfaith Hospital are the major voluntary detoxification units in New York. Morris Bernstein Institute probably serves more addicts in a single year than any other hospital or agency in New York and, perhaps, the nation. During 1966 they served more than 9,000 different addicts, many two or three times. Services are broad: detoxification, related and nonrelated medical treatment, methadone maintenance stabilization, and an induction center for New York City's Phoenix Houses.

After detoxification centers the next most frequently mentioned treatment facilities were hospitals such as Manhattan and Pilgrim State Mental Hospitals, Riverside, and Lexington. Another third (32%) of our sample said that they had previously been in this type of drug treatment. Prior to the enactment of the present civil commitment program in New York, narcotics treatment was undertaken in eight mental hospitals, as described earlier; these account for the majority of those who said they had been to hospitals for treatment. Ten and 4% of the men, respectively, reported being at Lexington and Riverside.

Self-help therapeutic communities were cited by only a small percentage, only 3%, but there were only two such communities in New York before 1967—Daytop and Odyssey House. Only two persons from the whole sample had been to Synanon.

The motivations of addicts for going to rehabilitation programs are similar to, or perhaps only a little different from, their motivations for going to detoxification. The addict goes to a treatment program to obviate some pressure in his environment. If he does not go to manage his tolerance, then he goes to appease someone in a position of authority over him who demands it, a spouse or family member or, most recently, the demands of a welfare policy that accepts addicts only if they participate in some treatment program. They also might go for treatment because of real or expected threats from the police or the street. If an addict is a pusher or dealer, the street may have become so hot that he will go to treatment to avoid an expected arrest. Then again he may have taken off the wrong person and someone in the street may be looking for him to even the score.

After an individual gets to treatment and stays awhile he usually gives up any previous commitment he has made to stay with the treatment, to "cure" his habit or rehabilitate himself, and leaves the hospital or treatment center and either immediately reverts to heroin use or gradually drifts back to it. When the parole or probation officer is satisfied he is helping himself, when his family is off his back, when the neighborhood has cooled or his habit is reduced, the addict usually returns to the street and drug use. Only occasionally will the addict genuinely wish to give up drugs and make a concerted and whole-hearted attempt to give up heroin; and even then he may abstain only a little while and then relapse.

Being perceptive and sensitive to other persons' expectations and needs, addicts learn to tell persons in treatment and detoxification programs what they expect to hear. As one particularly candid black man put it:

> How can you tell that pretty social worker who would like to think she is going to help you to get off drugs, to cure you, that you can't get high anymore and you'd like to reduce your habit so that you can enjoy dope again? How can you tell the social worker that you are just tired of having your family complain and want to get them off your back?

[6]

New York's Big Push

During 1965 and 1966, addiction and the crimes associated with it became a major political issue in New York, at both city and state levels. Incumbents and aspiring candidates for mayor and governor came up with plans and counterplans for treating and controlling narcotic addicts. Reports of plans and strategies appeared regularly in newspapers, and debate was heated but not particularly wide-ranging. "Needle Park," located at 73rd Street and Broadway and earlier a popular meeting place for addicts, became the site of many a campaign speech. Not since the Harrison Act of 1914 had addiction held out such prospects for publicity among politicians.

THE NEW YORK CITY PHOENIX HOUSES

Mayor-elect John V. Lindsay proposed a coordinated, comprehensive plan for treating and controlling addicts. A constant theme in the presentation of the plan was the need for coordination and cooperation between existing programs and new ones. Such comprehension and coordination was never attained.

The mayor's bias in the realm of treatment was toward therapeutic communities. The previous mayor, Robert Wagner, had been responsible for the detoxification units at Morris Bernstein Institute and Metropolitan Hospital and initial funding of the Dole and

94

Nyswander Methadone Maintenance programs. These were, in effect, Mayor Wagner's programs. Any programs for which the new mayor could take credit would have to be different from the previous mayor's. They were.

The development of the therapeutic communities was the responsibility of Dr. Mitchell Rosenthal, a dynamic but sometimes very authoritarian psychiatrist who had successfully developed a Synanon-type therapeutic community of mental patients in the Navy. Dr. Rosenthal, known to staff and residents alike as Mitch, with ex-addict Pete Falcon and 12 addicts recruited from the Morris Bernstein Institute, opened the first facility in May 1967 on 85th Street between Broadway and Amsterdam, right in the middle of one of the areas of high drug use on New York City's West Side.

Since these early beginnings, Phoenix House, under Dr. Rosenthal's direction, has grown steadily. As of April 1971 there were 1,150 persons in 14 houses (the basic treatment unit of the program is usually a brownstone or tenement building with 65 to 80 residents). This growth was not as Dr. Efren Ramirez had claimed it would be, but he was rather unrealistic in his claims. It took Synanon ten years to get their population up to 1,000; Phoenix Houses built a similar population in a little over three years.

Very briefly, the essential idea of the Phoenix House program is that ex-addicts are employed to reeducate and resocialize the addict to deal with his life and problems. Addiction is conceived of psychologically as being not the cause of the addict's problems with society but as a symptom of greater psychological problems that have resulted in a character disorder. These problems are explored in an often violent but always compassionate confrontation group therapy called "encounters," held three times a week.

The resident's life in the therapeutic community is active and well structured. There is little time for boredom and no one is ever allowed just to lie around or engage in reverie. The treatment process goes on 24 hours a day and each person is expected to be actively involved in his and the other residents' rehabilitation. From the first morning meeting until the resident goes to bed at night, he is expected to give completely of himself to the community.

Work and an elaborate system of rewards and punishments are utilized by the communities to educate and socialize the addict. He must earn his way in the house; there are no particular rights or privileges. Everyone who enters the community starts at the most menial tasks, usually on clean-up crews, and is expected to work himself up an elaborate hierarchy of jobs that can theoretically (but in reality only seldom) lead to becoming director of the house. At each step and on each job the resident must prove himself and work to his capacity. If for some reason he does not, it is seen as the responsibility of the other residents to confront him with his actions or attitudes and demand that he change.

Residents continually observe and comment upon the behavior of others. Each person is expected to assume the responsibility of enforcing every rule and every norm of the community. "Responsible concern" for other persons within the community is expected of everyone; should someone observe another person breaking rules or expressing "negative attitudes" and fail to report it, he will be punished along with the rule-breaker. In other words, the street codes that call for keeping confidence against nearly all authorities are actively fought; to be a "responsible" resident according to the program ideology one must be ready to report and criticize others.

All privileges, from telephone calls and passes to single rooms, must be earned through the progress made in the community. Nearly all behavior is seen as therapeutic or potentially therapeutic. "Good" attitudes and behavior, hard work, and conscientious concern are rewarded; "bad" attitudes and behavior are punished by demotions, extra work, and in some cases by ostracism. Both reward and punishment are elaborately devised to fit the needs of the individual and the situation.

In many respects, the techniques used by Phoenix House and other Synanon-modeled therapeutic communities are similar to those used by the Red Chinese to "brainwash" captured prisoners of war in Korea, and particularly those used to reeducate and resocialize Chinese university students and faculty members during the 1950s. Robert Jay Lipton's study of these techniques in his book *Thought Reform and the Psychology of Totalism,* published in 1961, shows specific similarities in the use of criticism of self and of others and in the elaborate use of the community and group pressures to force the subject to accept the values of the group and change his behavior. Seemingly the only differences between the two techniques are ideological.

The use of an ex-addict staff overcomes much of the failed communication that often develops in professionally run treatment programs. Leadership, or a good part of it, arises out of the community, and most everyone is expected to assume leadership in any number of ways. As a result, the community tends to run itself without unnecessary or overburdening external authority. There are no guards or persons who keep security in Phoenix Houses.[1] Residents take over these functions completely. And despite the fact that most major decisions eminate from a small group of paid staff members and are made in an often autocratic manner, residents express the idea that the community belongs to them. There is, if nothing else, an illusion of democracy created in Phoenix Houses.

The general atmosphere within Phoenix Houses is exciting. Residents are outgoing and actively friendly; this is part of their retraining, but it soon becomes a genuine part of them. They are taught to explore their self-awareness, to increase communication with others, and to overcome whatever blocks or inhibitions may have impeded their functioning. There is a genuine concern for others that goes far beyond the usual ideas of fellowship and brotherhood. Residents are expected to criticize and confront everyone in the community, especially those they like best or are closest to.

In some ways Phoenix House is much more wholesome, more moral, more ethical than the greater society and so is in many ways utopian. Residents live among persons who express concern for each other, which is far different from the harsh and competitive world outside of Phoenix House. It was, however, created to treat and rehabilitate addicts; and as it uses public monies for this purpose one must ask how effective it is in attaining its goals.

Program Effectiveness

During the summer of 1968 our project interviewed 157 persons at two Phoenix Houses. Most of our samples were males (132) from 205 West 85th Street, the first Phoenix House, and from Phoenix I at Hart Island. There were major differences in the two houses. The residents of 85th Street were, with only a few exceptions, persons who volunteered for the program, while most of the residents of Hart Island were convicted felons committed to the New York State Narcotic Addiction Control Commission and placed in the Phoenix House program through a special induction in the city prison at Rikers Island. At the time of our interviews there were only a few women on Hart Island and none in Phoenix I, so in order to include women we interviewed all the women then on

1. At Hart Island there was a token security force whose function was almost completely preempted by residents. This security force checked persons on and off the ferry and was only on the Island to satisfy an agreement with the Department of Corrections.

Hart Island, a total of eight. There was a similar problem with teenagers, so we also interviewed everyone under 21 at Hart Island.

Each of the 157 was followed with periodic record checks to
chart his progress in the program and determine the effectiveness of
the program.[2] These checks were made after 12 months (September
1969), 16 months (January 1970), and 23 months (August 1970).[3]

At the first record check made in September 1969, we found
that two-thirds (66%) were still in the program, while a third (34%)
had "split" (left the program) against advice; this was after 12
months. At the second check, 16 months from the original interview, the percentage remaining in the program declined to 46%,
while 54% had split. After 23 months we found that three out of
five (64%) had left the program and were considered splitees, while
one in five (22%) had completed treatment and was considered a
graduate. Of the remaining 14% still in the program, half (6%)
were considered "elders," a status in Phoenix House that gives the
individual considerable responsibility in the program and at the
same time allows him the freedom of leaving at night and on weekends. Of the 12 persons (8%) still in treatment after 23 months, four
were persons who had previously split the program, reverted to
drug abuse, become readdicted, and returned to the program.[4]

Graduates

All but two of the 35 persons who had graduated from the
program by August 1, 1970, had been drug free and made a good
adjustment to a life of abstinence. Most were working in Phoenix
House or for the outreach programs of the Addiction Services
Agency. Working for the program, or the provision of a future job
in the program, has been part of the program ideology and has
caused some persons, myself included, to criticize Phoenix House.

Phoenix House, like Synanon, does not allow persons to return
to the larger community as it should. In the original plans of the

2. Admittedly record checks are a limited way of determining the effectiveness of a treatment program. Ideally one should conduct individual interviews
supplemented by some reliability check such as urine analyses. This was our
original plan, but we were unable to realize this design when funds for the
follow-up were curtailed. As limited as record checks are, they do give a general
picture of who leaves and who remains in the program and each person's status.

3. Most of the information in this evaluation comes from the article au-
thored by myself, George Nash, Kay Foster, and Ann Kyllingstad, "The Phoenix
House Program: The Results of a Two-Year Follow-up" (Mimeographed, 1971).

4. Persons committed to the program may leave but may also be picked
up on a warrant and either be returned or sent to a state facility.

program a reentry phase was developed with the specific intent of easing persons back into the community, but this special phase was abandoned in 1970 when the program decided that reentry was not working as they had expected.

Since its early beginnings, and particularly during its rapid growth, Phoenix House has tried to fill jobs within the program from its own residents. This, I believe, is understandable, since so much of life in a therapeutic community is a sort of job training, and it is far easier and perhaps more efficient to use persons trained in their own program. But Phoenix House has *not* developed viable alternatives to working in the program. They have *not* developed job training or used existing job training programs as they could or should. They have *not* encouraged persons to return to school or go on to college. In fact, there are very obvious anti-intellectual and anti-education attitudes in Phoenix House. This is particularly unrealistic for the younger persons in the program.

Eventually, as the program's growth stabilizes, graduates will of necessity have to go outside of the community for jobs. They should, however, be making plans for that eventuality now and encouraging graduates to work outside and to leave the program.

Splitees

Not unlike Synanon, Phoenix House gives little consideration to those who leave the program. Once someone leaves he is considered a splitee, and for all purposes he is lost to the program. In the overstatement of some residents and staff members, "He is considered dead." No efforts are made to give the splitee any assistance after he or she leaves; no efforts are made to get him to another treatment that might be more effective for him. Everyone is expected to fit the mold of Phoenix House, and if someone cannot make it, then nothing else is considered.

Much of this has to do with the general attitude in Phoenix House that the therapeutic community modeled after Synanon is the *only* effective way to treat addiction. So much energy is put into believing in the efficacy of their program that they close their minds to other programs. This attitude holds from Mitchell Rosenthal down to the most recent director. Such a belief denies the fact of other programs.

Those who leave the program are accepted back again but only after they are given severe and demeaning tests. Only a small percentage of our sample (4%) returned to the program after leaving.

Splitees are most reluctant to return to the program after they leave.

In our effort to elaborate on our record-check evaluation of Phoenix House, we also made follow-up interviews with 33 splitees and contacted the families of four more we could not reach. Eleven of the follow-up interviews were from a small random sample of 14 persons selected from all the splitees as of August 1970. The remaining 22 were persons we had contacted after the first record check and were by no means chosen at random; they were persons who were easy to contact—who responded to letters or were easily located at known addresses, in other treatment programs, or in jail.

Of the random sample of 14 followed up in August 1970, we learned from actual interviews with the individuals that four were at that time readdicted and using heroin on "the street," one of the 14 had been readdicted and was in prison, two had been readdicted and were in other treatment programs, and *four were drug free* and leading stable, productive lives.

Of those persons whom we did not find, interviews with relatives disclosed that one was in prison after readdiction, another was readdicted and "on the street," and the family of the third did not have any knowledge of his whereabouts or whether he was addicted or not. Summing up, of the 13 for whom we had information four were drug free and nine had relapsed and become readdicted.

The 22 nonrandom interviews with "splitees" support the findings of the small random sample. Nearly a third (7) of the non-random group were abstinent at the time of the interview, while two-thirds (15) had reverted to drug use (six were interviewed "on the street," six were in state facilities, two were in the Harlem Hospital Methadone Maintenance program and became readdicted after leaving Phoenix House, and one was reported by his family to have become readdicted and then to have gone to Synanon). I should, however, caution the reader that all of these persons were those who were easiest to find, who were in treatment or doing well for the most part, and that any generalizations would be limited.

Analysis

Analyzing the data on outcome, we found that age was one important factor; another was how the individual came to the program—whether as a volunteer or through criminal certification. Neither ethnicity nor sex were related to staying in the program; women stayed in this program as often as men, and there were no differences between blacks, whites, and Puerto Ricans.

Motivation would seem to be the reason for differences between volunteers and those committed to the program. Criminal commitments, in every case, came from a special induction program at New York City's Rikers Island, a medium-security jail. Many joined the program to get out of jail, and some said they planned to split the program at the first opportunity. Many did just that.

As I explained earlier, volunteers to treatment programs are not always as voluntary as it would appear superficially. Not everyone who volunteers for a treatment program wants to give up drugs. Most who volunteer for treatment go under some duress, some pressure, so the motivations of volunteers are not as pure as one might think. There was, however, no legal commitment binding volunteers to the program. Volunteers did stay with the program longer than criminal certifications; after 23 months 40% of the volunteers had either graduated or were still in the program, while only 27% of the criminal certifications were in that category.

Another consideration in these differences is the facility in which most of the criminal certifications were treated. Most of the certifications resided on Hart Island when we interviewed them, and many stayed there for a long period. Criminal certifications on Hart Island often resented the ways that they were treated in the program. In many instances they had to stay in the program longer than volunteers before they were given privileges. Time spent on Rikers Island was, contrary to what they were told, *not* counted as time in the Phoenix program. Many persons had spent as long as 12 or 18 months on Rikers Island waiting to get to Hart Island; they resented the way the program discriminated between volunteers and certifications. In all fairness, the program either should not have discriminated between the two groups or should not have taken the criminal certifications in the first place.

Age, the next most important variable, had a considerable effect upon the resident's ability to remain with the program. Those under 21 years of age tended to leave the program far more frequently than those older. Nearly three out of four (73%) of the 41 persons in our sample who were under 21 had split the program by August 1970. Those over 21 did much better; only 58% of this group split, while the remaining 42% were graduated or still in the program.

This outcome was contrary to our expectation. Those of us who made the evaluation had originally expected that young persons, because of their short drug histories and seemingly lesser entrenchment in drug and criminal cultures, would do better in

Phoenix House than older persons, who had longer histories of drug use and stronger criminal and drug associations.

As I think about the possible reasons why older persons might do better in Phoenix House, several come to mind as plausible. The first is the motivation to remain drug free. It would seem that older persons, because they have experienced more of the hardships associated with heroin use—being arrested and sent to jail, overdosing, being rejected by family and friends—would be more willing to give up heroin use to obviate these hardships. To the young, the antiheroic aspects of the life of the addict may still appear glamorous.

The program itself is long and often difficult. The length of time seems to increase, not decrease, and some persons cannot withstand the personal revelations and constant confrontations that are demanded by the program. Older persons, because they have lived longer and have experienced more of life and its hardships, are more willing to stay in the program and give up immediate satisfactions. The young, on the other hand, have brighter prospects; they have their whole lives to live and are anxious to experience life—to get a job, own a car, have a girl—and split the program to get busy living.

Additionally, the demands of the program may be more easily met by older persons. Residents in Phoenix House are expected to assume considerable responsibility and take leadership roles; older persons, as they are apt to be more mature, may have an advantage over young persons in these activities. In some respects the expectations of Phoenix House may be unrealistic for young persons. For an example, one 14-year-old boy who was perhaps also mentally retarded was often admonished for acting like a 14-year-old. Young persons may find that they cannot live up to the community's expectations.

Reviewing the findings, I find that Phoenix House is only successful with a small minority of addicts. Twenty-three months after the initial interview one in five (21%) had graduated and remained drug free and 14% were still in treatment. Of those who left the program against advice, three out of ten (29% of 14 persons) were drug free, working, and leading stable, productive lives. Furthermore, a recent study by the New York State Legislative Commission found that only 79 of 2110 admissions to Phoenix Houses during 1967–1970 had completed the program; this is a completion rate of only 3.7%.[5]

5. Legislative Commission on Expenditure Review, *Narcotic Drug Control in New York State, Program Audit Highlights* (Albany, New York: 1971).

THE STATE PROGRAM

At approximately the same time that the City was selling its program, Governor Nelson Rockefeller proposed, and the New York legislators passed, a law to establish a "comprehensive" program of civil and criminal certification to control narcotic addicts. During Rockefeller's campaign to sell the program he used the usual tactic of politicians when dealing with addicts. He played upon the public's fear of addicts and the crimes they commit. He sought to assuage these fears by assuring definite control of the addict—by getting him off the street and into treatment so the citizenry could live without threat of theft or burglary.

Civil certification was not a new idea. Ever since the upsurge in the incidence of addicts in the 1950s there has been a general movement among the states to establish civil commitment laws for narcotic addicts along the lines of those established for the mentally ill. Twenty-two states and Washington, D.C., have at some time or another in the last 20 years had civil commitment laws that dealt with addicts, but only two states have established specific programs for treating committed addicts—New York and California.

New York, under the Department of Mental Hygiene, began to commit addicts civilly to state mental hospitals in 1960, but it was left to California to enact the first broad civil and criminal certification laws and a special program for treating addiction.

The California laws began as a conscious campaign to change the general criminal status and definition of the addict that had resulted from the Supreme Court decisions of 1919 and 1920 that, though never formally, made addiction a criminal activity. This campaign began in 1959, was led by a Southern California radio station, and culminated in 1961 in legislation. The legislation specified two types of commitment, civil and criminal, and a special program of treatment under the California State Department of Corrections.

During September 1961 a treatment program under the supervision of Roland W. Wood began without facilities or staff. Temporary facilities were established in the same year, as was a staff, and in 1963 the program found permanent facilities at Corona Rehabilitation Center (CRC) near Riverside, California.

The 1961 law stipulated that persons committed could be held in treatment for two and a half years if civilly committed and seven years if criminally committed. The time spent within the treatment facility is variable, but the first stay is usually nine months. The general objective of the program is the control of drug addiction, to be achieved by isolating the addict in treatment which, according to program staff, includes: a regime of group therapy in very large groups, general education and vocational training, spiritual guidance, and discipline and restraint, followed by close supervision in parole while the addict is in the community.

CRC, the principal facility of the California program, is in many respects like a medium security prison rather than a treatment program. You may perhaps call it rehabilitation in the prison sense, as its title implies, but you certainly cannot call it treatment in the medical sense. Security is very much an important element in the program—double cyclone fences surround the facility, with armed guards in watchtowers—and there is a strong corrections approach within the facility. The approach is single-minded, meaning there is only one approach, with little effort toward developing different treatment modalities for different addicts. Treatment in CRC is secondary to the effort of controlling the addict, but the Center has created a relatively humane and reasonable environment within the framework of a corrections facility.

The California program is only a little more effective than that of Lexington and Riverside Hospitals. John Kramer, the former Chief of Research at Corona and now an outspoken critic of commitment programs, found that 35% of 1,209 persons were in "good standing" (had not been returned from parole after a single stay in treatment) one year after their first release from the treatment facility. This declined after three years to 16%.[6] Recently Dr. Kramer said of the California program:

> One can only conclude that the California Civil Addict Program successfully rehabilitated only a small minority of the narcotic addicts committed. This raises the question of whether the limited degree of success achieved is sufficient to justify the length of incarceration of the many who do not respond to the program. It is also worthwhile to enquire if perhaps other approaches might not be more successful without depriving so many of such a great amount of personal freedom.[7]

6. John C. Kramer, with Richard A. Bass and John E. Berecochea, "Civil Commitment for Addicts: the California Program," in *The American Journal of Psychiatry* (1968).

7. John C. Kramer, "The State Versus the Addict: Uncivil Commitment," in *Boston University Law Review*, Vol. 50, no. 1 (1970).

New York State has, in general, taken over most of the elements of the California program: the idea of control, general treatment regime, and emphasis on correction and security. The laws of both are similar, except that terms of custody are much longer in California. Treatment in New York is organized under a separate control commission rather than under the Corrections Department.

The appropriation for the New York program was unprecedented in its generosity. Between 1966 and 1971 the state legislators gave the program more than $288 million. During the first year of the program (1966–1967) the appropriation was $3.6 million, an increase of $900,000 over the 1965–1966 budget. The second year (the first operating year of the program) saw an increase to $54.3 million. Money continued to be provided for the next years: $73.4 million in 1968–1969, $76.5 million in 1969–1970, and $80.5 million for 1970–1971. There was certainly a large commitment on the part of the state and more than enough money to operate the program.

Under the terms of the law, a four-man commission headed by Chairman Lawrence W. Pierce was established to plan and implement a comprehensive treatment program for addicts. In broad terms, the legislation gave the state and its citizens the power to request certification to the custody of the Commission of any narcotic addict or person in danger of becoming an addict. After a medical examination and hearing or a jury trial, if requested, persons were certified as civil certifications for an indefinite period up to three years and as criminal certifications (for persons convicted of felonies) for an indefinite period not to exceed five years.

The first facility opened in April 1967; during the first year 3,600 persons were certified to the program. This number increased to 4,100 by December 1968 and 4,400 by April 1969. By the end of 1968, the year of our first interviews, the Commission was committing addicts to eight of their own facilities, eight units in state mental hospitals (all but one of these, Manhattan State, were closed during 1969), five units in state correctional facilities, and Phoenix House on Hart Island.

We investigated six of these facilities: Bayview, Edgecombe, Woodbourne, Manhattan Rehabilitation Centers, the narcotics unit of Manhattan State Hospital, and Phoenix House at Hart Island. All but Phoenix House, which was covered earlier in the chapter, will be discussed here; Hart Island was part of the Phoenix House evaluation. Bayview, Edgecombe, and Manhattan Rehabilitation Centers were devised by the Commission as small, intensive drug treatment centers located within New York City. This was a break with the way California organized their program. The idea behind the New York facilities was to keep the addict in the community, close to his family and whatever resources he might have, rather than isolate him from the community. Manhattan State Hospital, a large hospital located on Randalls Island in the East River off of Manhattan, was operated by the Department of Mental Hygiene. Woodbourne was a larger, former corrections facility taken over by the Commission from the Department of Corrections and located approximately 100 miles from New York City in the "borsch belt." We did not include any of the Department of Corrections facilities in our evaluation, but visited each one.

The crux of the treatment in all facilities except Woodbourne was group therapy. Participation was mandatory in all facilities except Woodbourne. Therapy groups were generally led by counselors or Narcotic Rehabilitation Officers, except at Manhattan State, where doctors led the groups. Two facilities, Bayview and Manhattan Rehabilitation, were experimenting with the use of ex-addict group leaders. Techniques varied somewhat from group to group, depending upon the leader and his ability, but in general groups were modified encounter groups, with most of the confrontations coming from the staff rather than the residents. The material content of most encounters was less oriented to present behavior, as it was in Phoenix House, and more to past behavior and life history. As a result, encounters tended to be used more for psychological catharsis and less a person's day-to-day behavior.

One of the problems with therapy at Manhattan Rehabilitation, which we thought would also be present at other facilities, was that of quality and degree of participation and of certain breaches of confidence about emotional and personal material divulged in group therapy. Therapy did not involve the residents as it should have, and they soon learned what and how much to talk about to keep the group leader satisfied and to participate at a minimum. Information divulged in therapy was often used against the person giving the information by other residents on the floor, which caused many persons to think twice about what they said and to censor their participation. Consequently, women would "game" at saying what was expected or would try to make favorable impressions upon the staff and fail to participate in meaningful ways.

Education was the second most important element of treatment in the facilities studied. Educational programs varied in kind and quality: Woodbourne had a strong high-school equivalency program; Manhattan State, a good vocational training program (barbering, floor tiling, refrigeration, and so forth); Manhattan Rehabilitation emphasized basic education and vocational training for women. Except for Woodbourne and Manhattan State, education programs were slow getting started and were never, during our study, able to attain the kind of quality or participation necessary for a good program. Some persons did learn things in the centers, but most participated out of boredom—to "kill time"—or, in the case of Manhattan Rehabilitation, to socialize with other residents with whom socialization was otherwise restricted.

In many respects there was no real implementation of the basic treatment philosophy of Bayview, Edgecombe, and Manhattan Rehabilitation Centers. As the program operated, residents were not encouraged to use their own or the city's resources; they were not allowed to test themselves in the community while they were in treatment. The modified community health approach, as suggested by the relatively small facilities placed within the city, was never implemented. These facilities were run as if they were stuck off on an island, and for all intents and purposes they might as well have been. The only advantage I could see to the residents of these facilities was that it was easier for their families to visit them.

How Long?

The length of the first stay in all of the facilities except Manhattan Rehabilitation was usually nine months. This was a rule of thumb established by the Commission and was applied to almost everyone, whatever his job history or resources, age or family relationships. The Director at Manhattan Rehabilitation had kept women as long as 20 to 24 months during the first stay. Just prior to our record check to determine the status of everyone we interviewed, a policy directive from the Commission to Manhattan Rehabilitation allowed many of the women with 12 months in the facility to be released to aftercare. There was, however, one woman who had spent her whole time as a certification incarcerated. Early in her stay in Manhattan Rehabilitation she had led an escape attempt in which one of the NRO's was cut with a razor. After that she was held in the city's women's prison ("House of D") for six months awaiting charges, but these were dropped. After that she was sent upstate to Albion, a small corrections facility. When Albion was closed she was returned to Manhattan Rehabilitation, where she expected to stay for the remainder of her three-year commitment.

She was most certainly a difficult resident, but once the charges were dropped there was no reason to keep her as long as they did. The longer they kept her, the more bitter and recalcitrant she became.

Any second stay at a treatment facility (at our first interview 13% of the sample reported that they were in treatment for a second time) was usually three or four months in all, except for Manhattan Rehabilitation, where it was longer and more variable.

Aftercare

Upon release from the treatment facility, persons are sent to one of six aftercare centers; four of these are located in New York City. Aftercare usually consists of regular visits each week to the Center (less often if the client works regularly and does not exhibit drug abuse); periodic urine monitoring; and, for those who need it, a halfway house, day care, prevocational training, and group therapy. The major efforts of aftercare are to help the client to find a stable place to live and steady work and to control his drug abuse (through urine testing). Jobs are less of a problem than expected; nearly everyone found jobs but few held them for any length of time. Drug abuse was frequent—one center had more than 40% of its 350 clients receiving positive urine analyses during one week. When persons became readdicted they were either sent back to a treatment facility or detained for 14 days in a detoxification center (called "a 14 day play" by clients and staff). Many people stopped reporting to the center, and when this happened warrants could be taken out for their arrest.

The quality of aftercare varied from center to center and from one aftercare officer to another. Group therapy in aftercare was ineffective. Groups were led by aftercare officers who were in positions to use information gained in these groups against the clients. Naturally clients became reluctant to participate in a truthful way. Drugs were smuggled into and used in halfway houses. Many of the aftercare officers felt that the treatment facilities were such negative places that there was little they could do with the clients after they got out except help them stay out as long as they could. This was often done at the risk of censure or of being fired.

Results

In the only information made available by the Commission that even hinted at an evaluation of the effectiveness of their program, they claimed that 44% of 1,892 "rehabilitants" were returned to the community and placed on aftercare as of December 31, 1968, and had not resumed drug use.[8] Thirty percent ". . . were found to be re-using narcotics and were returned to rehabilitation centers. . . ." No mention is made of the remaining 25%, but I assume that many of these persons had absconded from aftercare, for which the usual reason is relapse to drug abuse—the addict simply stops reporting in order to avoid further detention.

This figure of 44% varies considerably from our data. We found that 13 months after our initial interviews (October 1969), when theoretically everyone should have had some opportunity to go to aftercare, only one in four (26%) of the 375 persons was in the category "good outcome"—that is, had gone to treatment and supposedly made some adjustment (since according to the records of the Commission they had not been returned from aftercare to a treatment facility). A similar number (27%) had escaped a facility, absconded from aftercare, or been sent to prison for some offense. Furthermore, nearly three out of ten (29%) had been returned one or more times to a rehabilitation center for some violation of the rules of aftercare, which usually are drug abuse or failure to report to the aftercare center.

How does this compare to other experiences with the commitment and treatment of addicts? California seems to be the most logical comparison, because it had served as the model for the New York program. You will recall that John Kramer found that California Rehabilitation Center was effective, with 35% "on parole" after one year and 16% after three years. CRC was clearly more effective than the five facilities we studied, with a difference of 9%.[9]

Actually, our data on "good outcome" is an overestimation of the general effectiveness of the five centers. Our study did *not* check the records of persons one year after they were released to aftercare, as Dr. Kramer did, but one year after the original interview. Persons in our sample could have been on aftercare for as long as 13 months or as little as one day. In our original design we had planned to make "time on aftercare" a factor in our analysis, but we were unable to carry out second and third record checks because of the curtailment of funds. As a result, more than half (52%) of all those

8. "Report of the New York State Narcotic Addiction Control Commission for the First Twenty-One-Month Period, April 1, 1967, through December 31, 1968."

9. In view of the sizes of their samples and ours, the variance is a statistically significant one.

persons who were in our category "good outcome" had been on aftercare less than four months.

Women at Manhattan Rehabilitation Center were out on
aftercare for a shorter time than residents from any of the other four
facilities. This resulted from a policy at the Center of keeping persons longer at the Center and a subsequent directive from the Commission that released persons just prior to our record check. Both
the time factor and the directive would tend to skew the results
toward an overestimation of "good outcome." With time, the percent is certain to decline. This was the trend in the California study
and is the general trend in all of the follow-up studies made of
treatment programs. A conservative estimate of this decline, when
time is considered, could be 6% but might also be higher. Assuming
a correction of 6%, I estimate that 20% of the sample of 375 would
be in the "good outcome" category after one year on aftercare. This
is considerably less than Kramer's figure of 35% and approaches the
15% figure he got after three years. This is, I emphasize, an estimate
after one year *only*. After two or three years, this percentage can be
expected to decline even further (the decline in the California study
from one to three years was 20%); it may reach as low as 5%, a
figure that is thought to be a natural remission rate for persons with
no treatment experience and, perhaps, only incarceration in jail.

Results by Facility

Individual facilities among the five we surveyed showed considerable variation in their effectiveness. Woodbourne, the relatively
high-security center, with the most obvious correctional approach,
was effective with only one in ten (10%) and had a failure rate ("bad
outcome") of eight out of ten (77%).

This would seem to be in keeping with the kinds of resentment
and hostility toward Woodbourne expressed to our interviewers.
Many residents, particularly civil certifications, felt that they had
been "railroaded" to a jail by judges and others working with the
courts, who sold ". . . a treatment program like a hospital" to them
or their parents. Criminal certifications, on the other hand, felt that
it was a reasonable place to "do time" and better than serving a long
jail sentence for a felony. Certainly Woodbourne resembled a jail:
residents lived in locked cells and guards (euphemistically called
Narcotic Rehabilitation Officers) walked around with clubs and
made no pretense at any function other than keeping security.

Interestingly, Manhattan State Hospital, with a rather free and easy atmosphere according to the residents, with a psychiatric orientation and very few security provisions, had a similarly low success rate (13%) and a high failure rate (77%). This is, however, not unexpected; Lexington Hospital, with a similar approach, has just as low effectiveness.[10] The most effective facilities were Bayview and Edgecombe, with similar success and failure rates (respectively, 23% and 64% for Bayview and 27% and 63% for Edgecombe).

Who Does Worst and Who Does Best

The older residents were, the less likely they were to respond to whatever it was (call it treatment, if you wish) NACC offered. Those over 26 years of age did worse in terms of "good outcome" (90%) than the two younger age groups. Those under 21 responded best (26% in "good outcome"). This finding accounts for the relatively better results of Edgecombe and Bayview, since these facilities had more younger addicts than the other two. This pattern appeared in all the facilities except Manhattan State, where the pattern was reversed: the oldest group had more "good outcomes" (21%), while the youngest did worst (7%).

The effect of age upon "treatment results" is easily understood. Age is related to both length of heroin use and the extent of criminality. Younger persons are less likely to be as heavily addicted and less likely to have been arrested or to have gone to jail than older persons. Many of the young were committed only because they were in danger of being addicted, not because they already were. Young persons more often maintained family ties and relationships and had more personal resources they could mobilize to help them. The older addicts, in many cases, had resigned themselves to lives of addiction and had few family ties and little or no resources to help them abstain from heroin use.

Race and ethnicity of residents also figure in the outcome of the New York State program. Whites, who made up 27% of our sample, responded best, while Puerto Ricans, who made up 29%, responded worst. More than one-third of the white group had "good outcomes," while only one in six (16%) of the Puerto Ricans were in that category.

One of the reasons for the generally low response by Puerto Ricans to treatment and rehabilitation was the exclusive use of

10. Henrietta J. Duval, Ben Z. Locke, and Leon Brill, "Follow-up Study of Narcotic Addicts Five Years after Hospitalization," in *Public Health Reports,* Vol. 98, no. 3 (1963).

English in both therapy and education programs in all facilities. Many of the Spanish-speaking residents we interviewed (in many instances the interview was done by a Spanish-speaking interviewer) had only a rudimentary knowledge of English and must have had great difficulty in understanding the subtleties of a therapy group conducted in English. To our knowledge there were no therapy groups conducted in Spanish in any of the facilities. This kind of insensitivity should not have been allowed in a program that supposedly expected to reach Puerto Rican groups.

In addition to this language barrier, Puerto Ricans are said to be reluctant to speak about intimate and personal problems among strangers. This is a cultural norm that is not easily overcome, especially in a group of strangers speaking a foreign language.

Whites, on the other hand, have not only a mastery of English but also more resources—better education, longer work history, more stable family groups—to assist them in making adjustments and doing well after leaving the facility.

Summary

Our study did not by any means cover all of the State facilities, but we did investigate a good cross-section of them. Some are undoubtedly better, and many worse, than those we studied.

Actually, none of the five facilities we studied is very effective in its treatment or rehabilitation of addicts. Major changes ought to be made in the State program. Unfortunately, in such matters as change the Commission seems to have become calcified at an early age and seems unwilling or incapable of devising different or innovative programs to meet the needs of different addicts.

If there is anything we know about addiction, it is that addicts are not all alike; one cannot generalize about them very easily. Somehow NACC does not realize this and treats nearly everyone alike—addicts and potential addicts, young and old, criminal and noncriminal, men and women. Up to now the principal criterion for placement in a facility (Bayview and Manhattan State excepted) has been available bed space; persons were and are sent to wherever there is an empty bed. From the onset the Commission should have assumed a more experimental attitude about their facilities and attempted to devise new and different ways to treat addicts.

Reading the yearly reports published by the Commission, one gets the impression of a number of different modalities in the ways the programs are operated—by the Commission, by the Department of Corrections, by Mental Health—but in reality they are nearly all alike. The only thing that is different among them is the degree of security. The various programs are *not,* by any means, new or original but often a renaming of existing prisons or hospitals.

As regards its own facilities, those conceived and operated by the Commission, it would seem that their only achievement has been to build another kind of penitentiary or jail. As one of our informants at Edgecombe explained:

> Do you know what this place is? It's a candy-coated penitentiary and nothing else.

They are indeed penitentiaries, albeit with group therapy and education, and they are no better and no worse than the penitentiaries into which society has been putting addicts since the Harrison Act. The results are the same also: a revolving door of incarceration, release, relapse, reincarceration, and so forth.

Civil commitment, as used by New York State, has turned out just as Dennis S. Aronowitz foresaw it in 1967 in the *Task Force Report: Narcotics and Drug Abuse* of the President's Commission on Law Enforcement and Administration of Justice:

> . . . an invidious method of achieving incarceration for a sickness which in and of itself cannot be punished criminally. . . . Civil commitment is but a euphemism for imprisonment.[11]

New York State should give up the hypocrisy of calling a "lock-up" program "treatment" or "rehabilitation" and cease to spend the taxpayers' money ($318 million up to 1972) on programs that obviously do not work. Civil commitment exists in New York only to keep addicts off the street, and, as far as I can see, there has been no real change in the way addicts are treated today than from before the law. The State has more power to incarcerate them but has done little more.

Why has the New York program failed? For one thing, the Commission was used to pay off political debts of Governor Rockefeller. The first chairman, Lawrence Pierce, and the first six commissioners were all political appointees of the usual pork-barrel variety. Only one of the six had any direct experience with addicts, and this experience was in the courts as an assistant district attorney. He was the most imaginative of the six but lacked the knowledge to set up a good treatment program. Perhaps an anecdote that he

11. Dennis S. Aronowitz, "Civil Commitment," in the *Task Force Report: Narcotics and Drug Abuse,* President's Commission on Law Enforcement and Administration of Justice (1967).

told himself may best describe his attitude toward the NACC treatment facilities. It seems a close friend's daughter had become involved with heroin and her family was afraid she was addicted. When the parents discovered her drug use they went to the commissioner to ask his advise about drug programs that the girl might go to. They asked about the State program, and he told them *not* to send her there because the program was not very good and advised them to send her to the City's Phoenix House program.

As in any other enterprise, good and intelligent leadership is important to the formulation of good drug-treatment programs. NACC did not have good leadership. Those responsible for planning and establishing the program were, almost to a man, unimaginative hacks. They had little if any commitment to their jobs and often feared and hated the people they were supposed to be treating. They held credentials and often had long experience but were incapable of inspiring other persons to do good work. They were not by any means villanous; they had good intentions, in most cases, but they did not have the imagination or knowledge to develop new and different programs. Commissioner Pierce was such a man; he could not and did not do the job. He left the Commission in 1969 under fire after Governor Rockefeller acknowledged that the State program had not accomplished its objectives.

Individual directors of State facilities came for the most part from established correctional and hospital treatment programs. Often they brought with them too many preconceptions and too much cynicism about addicts and as a consequence were never able to understand them. One such director never went near the residents of his facility after the initial months of the program.

In addition to this, the program was shackled by its civil-service status. Counselors, teachers, and NRO's were hired from civil-service lists, with little consideration given to their ability or commitment to treat addicts. Nearly all the NRO's, the staff members who had the most direct and constant contact with the addicts and who were considered to be crucial role models for the resident addicts, were recruited from among those who had passed a revised civil-service correction officer's test. All persons seeking jobs with the Commission at that level were required to take this test. Their expectations and attitudes toward the job were those of correction officers and they were given correction officers' identification cards, but the job in some facilities (Bayview, for example) was quite different from what they had anticipated. There they were expected to be firm, friendly role models to addicts who often resented the coercive nature of the program and acted out of that resentment. The job was quite different from the one they took the test for.

Some NRO's responded by changing their expectations and ideas about the job, but the majority did not. Most saw themselves as correction officers and wanted to remain as such. This confusion of job and title was crystallized when Bayview and other facilities asked the NRO's to turn in their correction-officer identification cards for NRO cards. Many of the NRO's refused to turn in their cards, with the explanation that ". . . they did not want to be made into some social worker type." As a consequence of this failure to specify and get acceptance of the role by the NRO's themselves, the "role models" at Bayview did not see themselves as role models, and the residents, in turn, did not see them as such and called them screws and cops.

At Woodbourne, there were no such problems. The correction officers of the previous corrections facility simply became NRO's of the narcotic rehabilitation center. The transition was quite easy; there was little or no change from one job to the other. The only change was in the sponsor—the NACC instead of the Department of Corrections.

Actually, treatment under civil commitment in most of the facilities of the New York program is synonymous with corrections. Under the guise of treatment, the State has found another way to lock up addicts. Fortunately, NACC's reputation as a lock-up program was quickly established on the streets. After the first year of operation addicts who genuinely sought treatment had learned to stay away from the program. The number of voluntary civil commitments has steadily declined since the program's first year, while criminal certifications have increased. The program is quickly becoming a refuge for persons who "cop" to being addicts rather than take prison sentences for a felony. It is far easier to do nine months in a NACC facility and return to the street than to do five or ten years in Attica, Dannemora, or Great Meadows.

[7]

Methadone Maintenance

A SHORT HISTORY OF METHADONE MAINTENANCE

In November of 1963 Dr. Vincent Dole of the Rockefeller University Hospital received a research grant from the New York City Health Research Council to explore new ways to treat narcotic addiction. One of the first things he did was to hire Dr. Marie Nyswander, a psychiatrist who had had extensive experience working with addicts, first at Lexington and then in various hospitals and clinics in New York City, and to give her carte blanche to develop new ways of treating addicts. Initially she set out to maintain two addicts on morphine within Rockefeller Hospital. This experiment showed little success as a method of treatment.

Both doctors decided that morphine maintenance was impractical and they withdrew the two addicts from morphine by substituting methadone. As the addicts were on large dosages of morphine, it was necessary to use equally high dosages of methadone, which were then increased to keep both addicts comfortable. Surprisingly, Dr. Dole saw a dramatic change in the addicts' behavior. When they were placed on methadone they no longer lay about impassively waiting for their next shot but became active and industrious. After this observation both doctors decided to experiment with methadone and maintained both addicts on a high maintenance dosage of methadone.

Methadone is a long-acting (36 hours), synthetic narcotic developed by the Germans during World War II as an analgesic when their original sources of morphine were cut off. With the United States occupation of West Germany the formula for methadone was seized and turned over to drug manufacturers in this country as an open patent. After the war Lexington Hospital developed a withdrawal technique that substituted methadone for heroin or morphine in gradually reduced dosages, and this method has been used extensively in hospitals since the mid-1950s.

Drs. Dole and Nyswander continued their experiments by injecting six addict patients with morphine while they were under the influence of methadone and discovered that methadone could serve as a block to other narcotics by preventing the high usually experienced. Additional medical studies on this small group also suggested that methadone, at the dosages given, had no deleterious effects upon the physiology or functioning of the individual.

With these six patients, a regime of treatment was developed that consisted of the stabilization of a maintenance dosage of oral methadone mixed in an orange drink, Tang, over a six-week period within the hospital. During this hospital stay the patients were moved gradually out of the hospital to work or school during the day and home during weekends. Each of the six patients was given close and intensive help through individual counseling in going to work or school as well as in attending to family, economic, and personal affairs. All of them made good progress and became stable, productive persons, some in only a matter of months.

Armed with these limited results, Dr. Dole went to Dr. Ray Trussell, the New York City Commissioner of Hospitals and now Director of the Morris Bernstein Institute, for funds to expand the program. Dr. Trussell was encouraged by Drs. Dole and Nyswander's tentative findings; he solicited and got $1.3 million from New York City to expand the program.

In March 1965 the expanded program moved into an open ward of the Beth Israel Medical Center (known then as Manhattan General) with its own staff and six new patients.

The program expanded rapidly; by October 1968, 1,139 addicts were in the program. With the expansion, firm criteria were established to include only those persons who were:

√ Between 20 and 40 years old (this was raised to 50 in 1968);

√ Addicted for at least four years and who had been under some other treatment and returned to heroin use.

Excluded were those:

√ With major medical or psychiatric problems (schizophrenics, for example);

√ Who came to the program under some legal compulsion to satisfy a condition of parole or probation.

The program was most definitely selective, but this selection was done more to satisfy a specific research design than to exclude broad classes of persons. Very quickly the program established a long waiting list, which also served to select persons who were either not committed to giving up heroin or who intended to use the program for objectives other than those of the program.

During the sixth year of the program the number of patients increased almost twofold; as of September 1969, 2,200 addicts had been admitted to the program through three different hospitals and were being served in numerous outpatient clinics.

PROGRAM OUTCOME

Our investigation of methadone maintenance consisted of extensive field visits at the Harlem Hospital inpatient stabilization ward and the hospital's three outpatient clinics on 125th Street in the middle of Central Harlem; interviews with a sample of 116 of the 289 patients in the program at the time;[1] and a record check 19 months after the interview to determine what percentage of the patients were still in the program.

The very first methadone maintenance patient came to Harlem Hospital in December 1965, and the program has grown steadily since then; at the time of our interviews there were 289 persons being treated and the plan was to increase the patient population by 100 each year.

All of the patients were male; female patients were treated separately at Morris Bernstein Institute. Three-quarters of the pa-

1. The sample consisted of three groups: one group of 49 long-term patients, all with at least two years in the program; a group of 53 most recent patients, all with less than nine months; and a third group of 14 who were being stabilized not in the hospital but as outpatients. Only the first two groups are used in this analysis.

tients were black (76%), 11% were Puerto Rican, and 13% were white. It is, in effect, a black program.

In general, our evaluation of the Harlem Hospital program supports the two Gearing reports on the progress of the program.[2] The record check of our samples after 19 months (August 1970) showed that only 16% of the 102 persons (ambulatory patients are excluded from these figures) had been discharged, while 84% were still in the program. Gearing reported in October 1969 that 82% of 1,554 persons accepted were still in the program.

Long-term patients, those who had been in the program two years or more at the time of the initial interview, did far better than short-term patients, those in the program six months or less at the time of the interview. More than nine out of ten (94%) of the long-term patients were still in treatment after 19 months, while three-quarters (73%) of the short-term patients were still with the program. It would seem that most of the long-term patients had settled down and could comfortably accommodate to the program rules.

One of the limitations, and perhaps a real shortcoming, of the reports made on the methadone program up to now is that information comes only from a single source, the records of the program. The evaluators have not gone to the patients themselves to learn at first hand about their adjustment. The original plan for our evaluation of the methadone program was to go to the patients themselves and expand the idea of "adjustment" developed by Frances Gearing's evaluations to include more than the simple enumeration of employment and arrest.

Physical Side Effects of Methadone

The most recurrent side effects reported by the patients of the Harlem Hospital program were excessive sweating and constipation. Most were bothered by excessive sweating, particularly during New York's hot summer months; two-thirds (66%) said they were bothered by sweating, with a third (36%) saying it was "a lot, now." This was indeed a problem for some. I recall that one patient had soaked through the front and back of his shirt during an interview in the middle of winter while I remained comfortable and, if anything, cool. Some patients experienced sweating as an initial

2. Frances Gearing, "Evaluation of Methadone Maintenance Treatment Program: Progress Report through October 3, 1968" and ". . . through March 31, 1969" (mimeographed, Columbia University School of Public Health and Administrative Medicine, 1968 and 1969).

side effect, but then gradually it diminished; 20% reported that they had been bothered in the past but were no longer.

Far fewer reported constipation as a side effect. A little over one in three (37%) mentioned this effect, but most (41%) said they had never experienced it; some (22%) had experienced it in the past but found it no bother "now."

The third most recurrent side effects (and perhaps the most important) was sexual—the loss of libido or difficulty in achieving an erection. More than two of every five (42%) patients said they had experienced this side effect at some time in their careers as methadone patients; 28% said that they were experiencing these problems at the time of the interview, 11% said that it bothered them "a lot," and 17% said "a little."

This side effect was reported by long- and short-term patients alike, which suggests that this is not just a problem of new patients that will subside with time. One man had had some serious reservations about the program when he experienced this side effect:

> Yeah, I had that problem when I first got in the program. I couldn't get a hard on for about a month. I had a lot of thoughts about getting off the program 'cause I'm not bothered all that much by heroin the way some people are. Well, it just sorta went away; I got no trouble now getting it up. But I wouldn't stay on methadone if it was going to hang up my sex life.

I think that this is something that Dole and Nyswander have neglected in their reports on methadone and should give more attention to. They could at least devise a small study of persons who report such problems and determine more precisely what the specific problems are and how they relate to methadone or the size of dosage. Perhaps all that is needed is some change in dosage; then again it may require personal or psychological counseling.

One of the myths held by addicts on the street is that methadone causes the user's bones and joints to ache, and many addicts put down the program for this reason. Of the 86 persons asked this question (the question was added after the interviewing began), only 13% reported such side effects, with 10% reporting them "now." The majority (87%) "never" experienced them. I believe that this effect is something that can safely be discounted, as most did not report it. The fears of street addicts arise out of their use of "dollies" on the street, with little control of dosage or observation by physicians. Under the controlled conditions of the Methadone Maintenance Program, such effects are experienced by a minority.

In addition to the user's experiencing only minor side effects, there are very few exterior signs of being high. Methadone is a powerful analgesic, and for most persons not on a regular regime the effects are obvious to the observer even though the high is blunted in comparison to that of heroin. Only a few methadone *patients* appeared to be under the influence of a narcotic. All of the interviewing was done by persons with considerable experience with drug users, and each was capable of detecting whether a patient was high or not. By far the majority (75%) of the patients were said not to "look high," with 15% "possibly high," and 9% reported "definitely high." Most of those reported "definitely high" by the interviewer were short-term patients or those stabilized on an outpatient basis. Long-term patients exhibited fewer visual signs of being high.

Family Relations and Happiness

Methadone maintenance seems to have a stabilizing effect upon the addict's family life. The fact that most of them no longer had to hustle (only 4% reported hustling) and were working (59%) or going to school (20%) seemed to temper their relationships with their families. Whereas while they were using drugs there were general disruptions in their family lives, this changed dramatically after they were on methadone. Nine out of ten (93%) reported that they got along "very well" or "fairly well" with their families and other relatives "now," while only 47% could say the same thing about the period while they were using heroin.

Most, I am sure, reported this because they themselves felt better about their own lives since they had become methadone patients. When we asked, "Is your life any better now than when you were using heroin?" the vast majority (95%) said "Yes."

Not only did they feel better about themselves, but they reported that they were generally happier than they were while they were using heroin. Nearly half (45%) said that they were generally "very happy," while a third (35%) said they were generally "pretty happy" "now" as methadone patients. Compare this to the period during which they were using heroin and you see a drastic change. Most persons (86%) reported that they were generally "not too happy" while they were using heroin, with a small percentage (10%) reporting they were "pretty happy" and an insignificant number (3%) saying they were "very happy." On the whole, their happiness while on methadone compares with the period before heroin use and is dramatically different from the time of use.

On this ground alone it would seem that methadone maintenance justifies itself. It does, however, have broader social benefits for the individuals it treats: there is a decline in hustling and criminal activities, and there are not only jobs but job satisfaction.

Effect on Hustling

Addiction is not by definition a criminal activity, but most urban addicts resort to a broad range of criminal and hustling activities in their search for drugs. Methadone patients are not particularly exceptional in this regard; nearly all (96%) reported that they had at some time been to jail or reform school for some apprehended crime.[3] In order to learn about the breadth of unapprehended crimes and hustling activities, we asked our sample of methadone patients the same questions about hustling that were discussed earlier, in chapter 3. Not unlike our other sample, methadone patients had been active in their hustling. More than three-fourths (76%) reported that they had sold drugs or acted as couriers during their careers in dope; nearly nine out of ten (87%) reported stealing; and more than a third (35%) had been involved with policy rackets. Everyone in the sample reported involvement with one or more of the seven hustling activities on our list.

This changes dramatically when addicts enter the program. When the same questions were asked of the patients in the sample for the period since they had been in the program, only 4% reported some hustling activity and 96% reported that they had been involved in none of the seven activities. This might be an overestimation of their good behavior, but there is no way of determining the reliability of the answers. A minority of persons do get involved with criminal activity while in the program. Dr. Gearing reports that 27% of the 122 black patients *discharged* as of March 31, 1969, were discharged because they had been arrested for some crime since they had joined the program.[4]

Some of these arrests are for the sale of drugs; this is the surest way of getting thrown out of the program. If a patient is arrested or in some instances even suspected of selling drugs, he is immediately discharged. From time to time a small number of patients do sell or give away a part of their supply of methadone, but there is not any

3. This percentage is considerably higher than for our sample of NACC males, which was 64%, and is higher than for blacks of that sample, too. In other words, patients in the methadone sample had been incarcerated more than those in our other sample.

4. This is 5% of all the black patients.

widespread sale of methadone from the program as many of its opponents have claimed. Early in our study we had heard that there were specific areas and corners in Central Harlem where liquid methadone like that used in the program at the time was being sold, but these rumors were unfounded.

I do know, however, of at least one person who confiscated methadone from the program and who probably sold it. I observed it myself. He put on a convincing act of drinking his methadone and then spit it out into an empty bottle, which he had in his pocket when I interviewed him.

This is, let me reiterate, the only instance we observed of anyone not drinking the methadone in front of the nurse. I suppose that some outpatients who receive several days' supplies or weekly supplies occasionally give away or sell some of their medication. The going price of liquid methadone is said to be $10 and some persons must be tempted to sell some of their supply, but they certainly must be judicious about it because they must look after their own need first. In any event methadone in New York City is seldom used to get high; most users prefer heroin to methadone because the high is more intense. Methadone is seldom a primary drug of addiction. Heroin is much too prevalent in New York for this to occur. Methadone, in whatever form, is almost always used to cut down the addict's tolerance or to keep his habit at a manageable level.

Hustling and criminal activities, by self-report, do fall off dramatically. Not that everyone becomes a model of solid citizenship, for human behavior is not so easy to change. Some addicts in the program probably do keep up their hustles and perhaps many more would if the program allowed them to. The program puts persistent pressure on the patient to change his behavior and does, in fact, get most people to change considerably. Program staff members, and particularly doctors and nurses, voice the program's expectations to the patient by threats of discharge and admonitions to keep clean for the sake of the program. These seem to work, for most persons come around to the program's demands for changed behavior.

Work and School

Pressures by the program on the patients to work or go to school are persistent. These begin early in the program, during the period of stabilization, and persist throughout the outpatient stage. Verbal reports of work by patients are substantiated by pay receipts and in some instances by telephone calls to patients at their places of work; but the program is reluctant to contact employers directly for fear of jeopardizing the patient's job. Unlike most parole systems, the program does not require that patients tell employers or prospective employers that they are in the program or former addicts. In the present climate of fear of addicts this would most certainly limit their chances for employment.

Patients are usually encouraged to take the first job they can find, work for three or four months to establish a work record, and then seek better jobs if they wish. Initially a good deal of time and effort was put into getting patients into school or job training, but this was not as successful as the program had expected. Currently the patient is expected to prove himself by working before he is helped to go to school. This is reasonable, because most patients have rather unrealistic expectations of their work potential. They all want to be computer programmers or operators, but most have little education and even less job training or skills. Some cannot manage the discipline needed to stay in school or to complete job training, and without some test of determination it would be impractical to send everyone to school right away. Despite a certain reluctance to send patients to school, more than a quarter (25%) had been to school since joining the program. Nearly all of these were long-term patients; half (48%) had been to some school since joining the program, with a third (36%) presently in school. Most of these were persons attempting to learn basic skills to pass high-school equivalency tests, but the participation ranged over a wide gamut of education from college courses to job training.

While most patients start in menial jobs when they first come to the program, after a period of time in the program a number do upgrade their employment to fairly satisfying, reasonably well-paying jobs. Methadone patients do not by any means become high-paid, glamorous, pop-industry executives, though some persons could. However, a sizable number have, since they came into the program, held better jobs than they ever had previously. More than a third (38%) said that their present or last job (since joining the program) was the best they had ever held. In many instances this would not necessarily be a good or meaningful job by middle-class standards, because most of the patients have had only sketchy work histories. In some cases where persons became addicted early in their teens they had had no *legal* work history at all. They may have sold drugs or become competent burglars, but they had never worked at a job that would be reassuring to a prospective employer. In many instances any job would be better than the previous "no job."

RECENT DEVELOPMENTS

The Dole and Nyswander Methadone Maintenance Program has been substantially expanded and changed since my investigation of the Harlem Hospital program. New funds from the New York City Department of Hospitals have expanded the number of clinics to 37, which could raise the number of patients to almost 4,000. There is now a new "rapid induction" program that has taken the stabilization phase of the program out of the hospitals into clinics. Addicts are being stabilized as outpatients. The age limit for the program has been lowered from 20 to 18 years, and a new, soluble methadone disc is used instead of the earlier liquid form. This last change was made because a child of a methadone patient unknowingly drank the Tang-methadone mixture and died as a result. This patient had been allowed to take a supply home and keep it in the refrigerator, and evidently the child mistook the methadone for an orange drink. According to the new system patients coming to the clinic must still drink the methadone in the presence of a nurse, but long-term patients in phases two and three now take discs home.

DISCHARGED PATIENTS

None of the recent changes in the program indicates that the program is doing anything to assist the discharged patients. Not unlike Phoenix House, which considers the splitee dead, the methadone maintenance program completely abandons patients who are discharged from the program. As yet only one attempt has been made to learn why patients in the program fail; this is a study made by Dr. Marvin Perkins and Harriett Bloch of 66 discharged patients. No efforts are made to assist them in any other way. The attitude of the methadone maintenance program is perhaps understandable in some ways, but it is unacceptable. One gets discouraged with people who do not take advantage of a good opportunity. At the same time this neglectful attitude toward dischargees reflects something of the greater society's moral censure of addicts. Rather than look for alternative approaches that might better serve these persons, the program simply cuts them loose.

In some ways the program sends some of their discharged patients to an early death or certain imprisonment. In the follow-up study of 66 discharged patients made by Dr. Perkins and Harriett Bloch, it was discovered that 6 (9%) had died and 72% had been incarcerated since being discharged. This is an extremely high death rate; it is more than 5 times the death rate for similar age groups in New York City. The incarceration is also high even for addicts. Certainly some alternative treatments ought to be considered or devised to assist these "treatment failures" for purely humanistic reasons, if for nothing else. Addicts should not be sent to early deaths simply because they cannot resist drug abuse or abide by the rules of the program. Lacking any other solution, these individuals could be maintained in the program on some provisional or "failed" status until some alternate approach is developed that can help them to make the necessary adjustments and to avoid drug abuse.

The same study also found that only two (3%) had been abstinent for any length of time (one for 16 months and the other for 46 months) after an experience in an abstention program, and another two were in other methadone maintenance programs. All but two returned to drug abuse after discharge from the program. In summing up these program failures, the authors state:

> The post-discharge course of 60 located heroin addicts who failed to continue in the methadone program appears to be in striking contrast to those who are reported as successfully maintained [on the program]. Death, criminal-legal involvement, incarcerations and hospitalizations, and continued drug abuse patterns would appear to be great risks for the group of failed patients. The authors believe that this evidence suggests intensified efforts to retain addicts may be needed in the methadone program. An alternative might be to the design of a new program for those who "fail." Perhaps both approaches should be undertaken.[7]

Another criticism of the Dole and Nyswander program is their seeming failure to provide for the long-range future of their patients and to give them some eventual drug-free alternative. As the program is presently conceived, patients may remain indefinitely in the program or until such time as they ask to be detoxified, which is usually viewed as voluntary discharge from the program. This could theoretically mean 10, 20, or 30 years of treatment. This decision for an indefinite period of treatment is based on the belief of Dr. Dole that prolonged use of heroin and other opiates may produce metabolic changes in the body of the addict that cause him to experience a drug craving long after he has been detoxified and is no longer

7. Marvin E. Perkins and Harriett Bloch, "A Study of Some Failures in Methadone Treatment" (Paper read at the 123rd annual meeting of the American Psychiatric Association, San Francisco, May 11–15, 1970).

subject to withdrawal symptoms.[8] This is a reasonable theory of addiction, perhaps no worse than other psychological theories (addicts have character disorders) and sociological theories (addicts use heroin because of their associations). But like these other theories, it has never been proven. There is as yet no evidence in humans of any metabolic changes occurring with opiate use, whether of heroin, morphine, or methadone, but many persons in the program assume its existence as the basis of their *modus operandi* and a few talked as if it had been proven.

I am not opposed to operating a program on the basis of theory or to having a theoretical approach, but I do balk at the way theories can often close peoples' minds to alternative approaches and stifle experimentation. Actually, the methadone programs are not the only ones that do this. To hear staff members at Phoenix House, Synanon, and other therapeutic communities talk, you would think they had completely solved all the problems of addiction and were the only ones who could treat it effectively. While Drs. Dole and Nyswander certainly do not take this position, they have closed the door and limited their alternatives by not developing collateral treatment along with methadone. Most particularly, they have not given those of their patients who have shown good adjustment and become stable, productive persons the alternative of being drug free.

Patients in the methadone program may upon request be detoxified, and a small number were detoxified and given voluntary discharges from the program. All, according to Dr. Dole, have experienced drug hunger and returned to heroin use, but none was given assistance in remaining drug free by the program; they were simply cut loose from the program and given no further help. That is not to say that they were not allowed to return to the program, because they *were* readmitted.

A much better approach would be to establish a distinct experimental program that would allow volunteers who exhibited good adjustment on methadone and wished to be drug free to get some continuing intensive support from the program during a trial abstention. Patients could perhaps be taught to recognize and handle their drug craving. Cravings or dependencies are not particularly unique to opiates. Those for opiates may be stronger, but there are several analogous dependencies experienced by many people—to-

8. For the best presentation of this theory, see Herman Joseph's article "Heroin Addiction and Methadone Maintenance" (mimeographed, Metropolitan Urban Service Training Facility, 1968).

bacco, alcohol, the sea for seamen, sexual relations, love affairs. To some extent people learn how to manage cravings for tobacco, for the sea, for a loved one by some substitute or distraction. Admittedly the craving for heroin is stronger, but perhaps people could be trained to recognize the impulse to use heroin and get support to resist it. Alcoholics Anonymous has done this for alcoholics with reasonable success; while I don't necessarily recommend that particular model, it does show that a craving can be managed when the drinkers make a commitment to give up alcohol and are given intensive individual and group support to do it.

Contact for such an experimental group would have to be close, perhaps more close than it is for phase one patients. They may have to live in a supportive community temporarily. Support may have to be available on a 24-hour basis and be responsive to the patients' immediate needs. When they do revert to drug abuse, help should be given to prevent their losing jobs or backsliding. Those who try but fail should be placed back on a methadone regimen.

Some methadone patients do express a desire to be drug free. Most persons talk in terms of the distant future, and when they have made good progress on methadone they ought to be given the opportunity to attempt it. It may be that such a program will not be effective, but I believe that methadone maintenance programs have a responsibility to attempt such an approach.

Only recently have Drs. Dole and Nyswander attempted such an experiment. In June 1971 they started a very small alternative drug-free experiment with 12 patients who had been in the program for three years, had shown particularly good progress, and wished to be drug free. It is much too early to expect results, but if this program is as well run as the regular program we can expect a reasonable presentation of the data. Of all the drug treatment programs, including Lexington, they have been most aware of the virtues of objective evaluation. Certainly some aspects of the evaluation could be improved upon, but they of all the programs have been amendable to it. One cannot say that of the State program, and only recently has Phoenix House gotten around to accepting evaluation.

8

Life Without Heroin

The commercial literature of addiction has been very explicit in depicting the day-to-day life of the heroin addict. Novelists, playwrights, and moviemakers have been careful to document the drama of the street life of the addict. Not all have been as realistic as they might have been, but several addicts themselves have given us good descriptions of the seeming magic and euphoria of heroin, the hustling, the daily struggle for money to buy it, the hopes of abstinence, and the lost hope of frequent relapse.

To the usual bourgeois the life of the addict seems horrendous, akin to that depicted by Hieronymous Bosch or, more recently, by Jerzy Kosinski in his nightmarish adventures of the outsider in the *Painted Bird*. What is less well known is that a good number of addicts do not see their life in these terms. The euphoria of heroin and the excitement of hustling serve many addicts in the same way that jobs, sex, and consumption serve nonaddicts.

If this is the life of the addict while addicted, what is his life like when he is not using heroin? Surprisingly, very little attention has been given by writers and researchers to this aspect of the addict's life. In fact very little is known about either abstention or relapse despite the voluminous amount of writing on addiction.

Nearly all of the research on abstention to date was undertaken in conjunction with the evaluation of various narcotic treatment programs. Consequently all were narrowly concerned with the enumeration of patients abstaining from heroin after the treatment and with the length of that abstention and little else. There has been only one attempt to learn anything about the specifics of the life of addicts during abstention; George Vaillant, writing in *The American Journal of Psychiatry* about 30 addicts abstinent for three years, found that high-school graduation, regular employment before addiction, and late onset of addiction were the best predictors of long abstinence.[1] Most were working and leading productive, happy lives, but more than half were substituting other drugs, usually alcohol.

Knowledge about the processes of relapse is only a little better. To date there has been only one attempt to learn anything of relapse after a period of abstention. This single effort was a very imaginative article by Marsh Ray that attempted to determine the forces that caused 17 addicts to relapse to heroin. He found that the tendency toward relapse after abstention occurred when the behavior of other persons who were important in the abstaining addict's life caused him to question his ex-addict status and see himself as being different from the nonaddict. Actual relapse occurred when such questioning by the abstainer was continual or recurrent and he began once again to define himself as an addict.

This dearth of knowledge and research on the processes of abstention and relapse is startling because it is the high incidence and recurrence of relapse after some treatment or abstention that makes heroin addiction the social problem that it is. In this chapter I shall attempt a preliminary and as yet exploratory description of certain kinds of adjustments made by heroin users during a period when they had voluntarily abstained from heroin.

INCIDENCE OF VOLUNTARY ABSTENTION

The use of heroin by most addicts over the course of their addiction is not a steady uninterrupted process, but rather a very periodic or episodic use. The beginning user may dabble in heroin for a long period of time, but once he becomes addicted and a tolerance for heroin has developed his use will be interrupted by pe-

1. Unfortunately for the methodology of the study only 17 of the 30 were interviewed. George E. Vaillant, "A Twelve-Year Follow-Up of New York Narcotic Addicts: Some Characteristics and Determinants of Abstinence," in *The American Journal of Psychiatry*, Vol. 123 (1966).

2. Marsh B. Ray, "The Cycle of Abstinence and Relapse Among Heroin Addicts," in *The Other Side: Perspectives on Deviance*, ed. Howard S. Becker (Free Press of Glencoe, Ill., 1964).

riodic detoxifications and by involuntary and voluntary periods of abstention in and out of jails and treatment facilities. One 42-year-old man whom we interviewed in Bayview had been addicted for 25 years; he said that he had lost count of the number of times he had "kicked his habit and been off heroin for a week or more," but it was at least a hundred times. In addition he had served 10 years (eight different times) in jails, during which times he usually was abstinent. At one time he was voluntarily off heroin for three years.

This man is obviously an extreme case, but many addicts did attempt to kick quite often. More than half (52%) reported that they had "kicked their habit and stayed off heroin for a week or more" four or more times, with a quarter (27%) reporting seven or more attempts. The mean number of times persons reported kicking and staying off heroin for a week or more was six times for the 422 men we interviewed. Many of these attempts are made simply to overcome a developed tolerance in order to get high again, but some are genuine efforts to abstain from heroin.

In order to document further some of the processes of abstention, we asked all the patients from our stratified random samples: "What was the longest period you've abstained voluntarily (outside an institution) since you started using heroin?" It is on this single, longest abstention that I have focused my attention and the following analyses.

Of the men we interviewed, two out of every five (40%) said they had voluntarily stayed off heroin (outside of a treatment facility or jail) for three months or longer, and one out of five (21%) had stayed off voluntarily for eight months or longer. Furthermore, 67 (16%) had abstained at one time for two years or more, 33 (8%) for three years or more, and 12 (3%) for five years or longer. One obviously middle-class man we spoke to had been off heroin for 13 years at one stretch and became readdicted after he was injured in an automobile accident and was given morphine by a physician to ease the pains of his severe injuries. After that initial injection he reverted to regular use, lost his job and family, and was eventually committed to the NACC program in lieu of a felony charge for sales.

Voluntary Abstention and Length of Heroin Use

These periods of voluntary abstention vary dramatically for age and length of heroin use. Abstentions of eight months or longer, which I have considered long abstentions, were reported by only 2% of the 127 persons under 21 years of age who had used heroin

four years or less, by 18% of the 57 persons from 21 to 16 years of
age who had used for 5 to 9 years, and by more than half (57%) of
the 93 persons over 26 years of age with 10 years or more of heroin
use.

This is contrary to Charles Winick's maturing-out thesis.[3] As
sociologists have observed that urban adolescents give up gang activity and its often associated delinquency when they mature, which
usually meant getting a job and a steady girlfriend, so did Charles
Winick observe that addicts seem to mature out of heroin use as
they reach, not their 20s, but their 30s. The evidence he offered to
support this thesis came from the listings of addicts made by the
Federal Bureau of Narcotics. When Winick analyzed their file of
inactive addicts (names of addicts were classified as inactive when no
reports had been sent to the Bureau for five years), he found that
persons who had been using heroin for ten years became inactive
around age 30. Winick did not know what happened to these persons nor did the Bureau. Some may have died, been incarcerated for
long periods, avoided further arrest but continued to use heroin, or
given up the use of heroin. There was very definitely a trend for
persons to become inactive, and his theory attempted to explain the
phenomenon.

Unlike Winick we found that length of heroin use is a better
predictor of long-term voluntary abstention than is age. In general,
the longer men used heroin the more likely they were to have had at
least one long abstention. That is not to say that age is not associated with long abstention for it is, but when age is held constant,
as in this analysis, the length of use is a stronger predictor of long
abstention. Among those who had used heroin for four years or less
the increases with age (2% for those under 21 years, 2% for those
from 21 to 26 years, and then a slight increase to 8% for those over
26) are only negligible. For those who had used heroin from 5 to 9
years and for 10 years or more the increases are considerably greater;
whereas only 7% of those under 21 who had used from 5 to 9 years
were abstinent, 24% of those over 26 years were. Similarly, there was
a large increase for those with the longest heroin use (10 years or
more)—from 44% to 57%. This suggests that, perhaps, the maturing
out of addiction and heroin use as reported by Winick may also be
more related to length of heroin use than age.

It may be that persons "burn out" of heroin use and addiction
after an extended period of use rather than mature out with age.

3. Charles Winick, "Maturing Out of Narcotic Addiction," in *U.N. Bulletin on Narcotics*, Vol. 14 (1962).

Rather than being the result of some life-cycle processes, a social and physical maturing out of addiction, getting off heroin may occur when the addict reaches some saturation level. At this saturation point, heroin use, hustling to get drugs, and going to jail and treatment become too much for him and he decides to give it up. This idea of burning out is supported by other data, which I will discuss more thoroughly in chapter 9, Rock Bottom.

Resources for Long Abstention

Rather surprisingly, the resources for long abstention turned out not to be class position or ethnicity but education. Persons who remained in high school and did not drop out had longer abstinences than those who dropped out. Nearly a third (32%) of those who finished high school had long abstentions, while only one-sixth of the dropouts (17%) had such abstentions. This pertains more to those over 21 years of age, since many more of the persons under 21 years of age had begun heroin use earlier and dropped out of school, the one often being the consequence of the other.

SELF-REPORTED BEHAVIOR DURING THE LONGEST ABSTENTION

Although the incidence of abstention is interesting as a phenomenon, the behavior of addicts during long abstention is far more important in helping us to understand something of the processes of abstention and relapse. And any understanding of addiction must take into account more of the actual processes of abstinence than have thus far been investigated.

The primary focus of this investigation of abstinence was upon reports of the addicts themselves concerning four areas—work, substitution of other drugs and alcohol, family relationships and associations with addicts, and general adjustments. Questions dealing with these areas were asked of the 163 persons who reported that they had at one time abstained from heroin for three months or longer.

Briefly, we found that the majority usually worked during the long abstention, did *not* drink heavily or use other drugs to excess, got along with their families, did *not* associate with other addicts or users, were *not* bored with their social lives, were usually happy, and were *not* treated like addicts by other persons.

Work

The single most interesting feature of the abstaining addict's life is the very high percentage who reported that they worked while they were off heroin; more than two-thirds (67%) said they usually worked at a regular job during that period, and 3% reported that they worked sporadically. Surprisingly, there were no ethnic differences in the reports of work; blacks and Puerto Ricans reported working as often as whites. This was despite the fact that black and Puerto Rican nonaddicts have much more difficulty finding and keeping jobs than do whites. This ability to get and keep a job occurred among persons who had little if any work history; many had given up work completely for hustling as an activity to get money or for any intrinsic satisfaction it might offer.

Drug Substitution

There is a general belief that most addicts when they give up heroin become alcoholics or use other drugs, such as barbiturates or cocaine, to excess. In an effort to determine the extent of substitution of alcohol and other drugs we asked all of those reporting three-month abstentions: "Did you drink heavily?" and "Did you use other drugs to excess?" When both questions were analyzed together—that is, to determine if the person did not use other drugs did he use alcohol, and vice versa[4]—we learned that roughly half used some substitute (51%) and half did not (49%). Of the two, alcohol was used by slightly more addicts than other drugs; 38% reported that they drank heavily at some time during the abstention period, while 27% said they used other drugs to excess.

Ethnicity figured in this substitution; Puerto Ricans tended to substitute some drug (62%) more than did whites (50%). Blacks substituted less (44%) than the other two groups. This pattern of substitution is reiterated for both alcohol and other drugs. Puerto Ricans and whites reported that they drank heavily and used other drugs to excess more than blacks did. These differences may be a result of the general tendency mentioned earlier for whites and Puerto Ricans to use more drugs, other than heroin, than blacks do.

Length of heroin use was also associated with the extent of drug substitution. Addicts who had used heroin for more than five years substituted more than short-term users and long-term users

---

4. Marijuana was not counted among the "other drugs."

drank heavily more than short-term users, but the differences between the two groups substituting other drugs were too small to consider significant. This difference is understandable; long-term users are more entrenched in their use of all drugs, they become dope fiends, and they may have to substitute some drug when they are not using heroin—as alcohol is legal they use that. This, while acceptable to society, is not always the best alternative for the individual. Excessive use of alcohol is in nearly all respects more dangerous physically for the addict than heroin use. But then again the alcoholic does not have to face the hostility of society's attitudes and laws that heroin users do. Alcohol is a legal, but often dangerous, alternative to heroin and opiates.

Family Life and Peer Associations

Whatever the importance of work and of staying off other drugs (some may even argue that neither are important), for the abstinent addict the real arena for adjustment is that of people— his family and peers. Very often the addict, while using heroin, does a good job of exhausting his family resources. The family is more than conscious of the addict's problems and his proclivity to relapse. During periods of incarceration or treatment, relations are often rekindled that have been strained, sometimes to the breaking point, during heroin use. The members of his family, out of familial duty or affection, wish to give him another chance, but they are guarded. As they are often the first victims of his addiction (most addicts steal from their families long before they steal from others) they become, perhaps, oversensitive to the addict and his behavior. They are quick to detect his previous failures, quick to see him slide back into his old behavior. This can, to say the least, create a lot of tension between the addict and his family.

Each of the respondents was asked questions about his family and peer relationships during long abstinence. The question that dealt with peers was asked from the belief that addicts would have a better chance to abstain from heroin use if they avoided associations with other drug users. Both questions were combined to indicate "good social relationships," defined as getting along with one's family and not spending much time with drug users. Nearly two-thirds (62%) had good relationships.

Good relationships were strongly associated with length of heroin use. Men with the shortest heroin use (four years or less) were more likely to have negative relationships, while those using heroin from 5 to 9 years had good relationships; long-term users (10 years or more) fell between the two. Probably the reason for this is that the short-term user still desired to use heroin and associate with other users. This association in turn alienates his family. The addict who has used heroin for longer times believes, because of his longer experience with relapse, that he must change his life and stay away from drug users. Those with the longest histories did not fit this pattern, though perhaps they, because of their long use and numerous failures to abstain, had resigned themselves to their addict associates.

General Adjustment

In order to get some ideal of the *overall* adjustments of each person during this period of long abstinence a scoring system was devised to assess each person's adjustment according to the four dimensions: work, drug substitution, social relations, and boredom.[5]

Each of the responses made by each person was given a score (0 for "no," 1 for "yes, sometimes," and 2 for "yes, usually") and the sum of all was taken.[6] These scores ranged from 0 to 16, 16 being the score of highest adjustment and 0 of lowest adjustment. All of the scores were divided into three groups for the purpose of analysis: scores 0 to 8 were called low adjustment; 9 to 12, medium adjustment; and 13 to 16, high adjustment.

Of the 160 persons scored in this analysis two out of every five (40%) were in the high adjustment group; a similar proportion (41%) scored from 9 to 12 and were designated the medium adjustment group; and the remaining fifth (19%) scored from 0 to 8.

Correlates and Resources of Overall Adjustment

Unexpectedly, neither length of heroin use (which was closely associated with drug substitution and family and peer relationships) nor ethnicity (which was associated with work) was associated with overall adjustment, but age, shown earlier as a powerful predictor

5. The question that asked, "Were you happy?" was excluded because it correlated highly with nearly all of the other items, and "Did people continue to treat you as if you were an addict?" was dropped because it seemed not to fit logically with the other items. This last item was, however, analyzed separately and is discussed at another point in this chapter.

6. Items 5 and 7 were given a weight of 2 because of the category groupings of the other four items.

of long-term abstinence, showed great differences. The youngest persons (under 21 years) were much less often in the high adjustment group (20%) than the other two age groups.

Unlike voluntary abstention, education was not particularly related to the addict's overall adjustment score, however, his compatibility with his family was. Nearly half (48%) of those who reported that they got along with their families "very well" before heroin use had high adjustment scores, as compared to a quarter (25%) of those who said they got along poorly or vacillated. Self-reported compatibility with his family before heroin use seems to be critical to the addict's adjustment during periods of abstention.

OVERALL ADJUSTMENT AND LENGTH OF ABSTENTION

During the development of the overall index analysis I asked myself what, if anything, should be the effects of "good adjustment." Should not good adjustment allow the individual to abstain longer? That is to say, long abstention is not just the result of some fortuitous circumstances but is affected by the individual addict's ability and efforts to make some adjustment to living without heroin. As I predicted, those with high adjustment scores had longer periods of abstinence than those with low scores; two out of every five (40%) of those with high adjustment scores were abstinent for *two years* or more, while only 16% of those with medium and low adjustment scores were abstinent for that long.

SELF-REPORTED HUSTLING

Hustling figures large in the urban addict's life. Most of those in our sample were forced by our existing laws and methods of control to hustle to support their habits. This situation changes dramatically when the addict gives up heroin and is abstinent. Hustling activities fell off markedly during long abstention; more than two-thirds (68%) of all those with abstentions of eight months or longer reported that they had not participated in any of the long list of activities that I reported in chapter 3, "Supporting a Habit." They did not sell drugs, cop for others, lend their works, run numbers, steal, pimp, or have sex with men for money. They might have done other things, because this list by no means exhausts all the possibilities, but they were not involved in these most recurrent hustles.[7]

Men who said they had good adjustments during long abstentions (those with high and medium adjustment scores) reported much less hustling activity than those from the low-adjustment group. More than three-quarters (76%) of those with high adjustment scores and 70% of those with medium scores said they had done no hustling when they were off heroin, while less than half (45%) of those with the lowest adjustment scores could report no hustling. Furthermore, nearly nine out of ten (87%) of those with low scores reported hustling before heroin use, while only half (48%) of the men with high scores did.

On the whole, hustling during abstention falls off sharply, especially for persons who have made good adjustments. Off heroin and adjusting to life without heroin, our respondents gave up most hustling activities. This definitely supports Alfred Lindesmith's arguement that addicts commit crimes to seek money for drugs and are not criminal in their general behavior.[8] Maybe those persons who find it difficult to adjust to society's norms and laws during abstention are more likely to be criminal. Certainly many more of them reported having hustled before heroin use than did either of the two groups that reported better adjustment.

BEING TREATED LIKE AN ADDICT DURING ABSTENTION

According to interpersonal theories of personality and social development, the individual's concept of himself and his subsequent role developments are dependent upon how significant persons in his social environment, usually family and friends, respond to him. Using this idea, we sought to discover from our abstaining addicts if the important other persons' responses (in this case being treated like an addict during a period of voluntary abstention) had any relation to their overall adjustment and to the length of their abstention from heroin.

7. As reported in chapter 3, the self-reports of hustling were very high: 81% said they had sold drugs or acted as a courier, 87% stole, 90% lent their works, 89% bought drugs for others, 28% pimped, 28% had sex with men for money, and 26% ran numbers.
8. Alfred Lindesmith, "Dope Fiend Mythology," in *Journal of Criminal Law and Criminology*, Vol. 31 (1940) and *Opiate Addiction* (Bloomington, Indiana: Principia Press, 1947).

More than two-thirds (70%) of those with long abstentions said that other persons did *not* continue to treat them as if they were addicts. Men who reported to the interviewers that they were treated like addicts during abstention more often had perilous adjustments (as reflected in lower adjustment scores) and shorter periods of abstention than those not treated like addicts. Half (50%) of all those who reported that they were not treated like addicts had high adjustment scores, while only 17% of those treated like addicts had high scores. One-third (33%) of those not treated like addicts had abstentions of 24 months or longer, while only one in six (16%) of those treated like addicts had similar long periods off heroin.

The cause and effect relationship in this analysis of overall adjustment is not by any means clear. It is difficult to tell which follows from the other. It could be that some were not treated like addicts *because* they made good adjustments, but I think that adjustment and the way others respond are interdependent.

It would seem that the added support of other persons, in this case by not being treated as a member of a despised group, gives the abstaining addict certain assurances that help him remain off heroin longer than those who do not get such support. This would seem to support Marsh Ray's theory that abstention depends on how other persons respond to the addict.[9]

RELAPSE

Addicts can make reasonable adjustments to square life and abstain, but this abstention is by no means always permanent or a safeguard against return to heroin. All of the men in this sample illustrate the addict's shaky abstention, for despite some long periods off heroin (16% were off two years or more) and relatively good adjustments, everyone I have been writing about had relapsed. All of the 163 men were in treatment because of recent heroin addiction. All were subject to some setback—such as the case of Eddy, a 42-year-old black man who became addicted when he was 26. His longest abstention was three years, from 1959 to 1962:

> I was doing well in Detroit. I was working regular as a plumber on tract houses. I had two cars, a '58 Bonneville and a '56 Olds. Well, I came back to a hell-hole, New York. I was okay; I worked for about a year in New York, then somebody breaks into my car and steals all my tools—$400 worth of plumbing tools. I couldn't work and

9. Marsh B. Ray, "The Cycle of Abstinence."

couldn't get a job then 'cause I had no tools. I got disgusted as far as responsibilities—getting a job and looking after my son. My father was nagging me to work.

I met this old girl friend one day; somebody I always wanted (sexually, you know). Terry, she had a lovely body. She told me she was using and she said she would save me a little taste. I shot up and it felt good. I had sex with her. I shot up just for a piece of ass. It was good though, the sex; and I went back looking for her the next day and the next day. Well, I found her and I started using again.

Returning to New York, losing his tools and his job, meeting an attractive addict girl were the impetus to send Eddy back to heroin, readdiction, jail, and eventually the treatment program in which I met him. For many, any one of the above reasons would have been enough to shake their adjustment and resolve to stay off heroin.

Our study did not attempt to learn any comprehensive details about the processes of relapse, and we asked only a single question, "Why did you start using heroin again?" Unfortunately, the answers to this too-simple question were superficial. Most persons cited psychological or emotional states such as unhappiness, depression, disgust, and boredom as the reasons for relapse. I did not then have the knowledge or the time to pursue the topic any further.

There are a number of general theories that attempt to account for relapse to heroin after an abstention but little real information about the subject. Traditionally, and perhaps logically, the assumption has been that personality factors, both those that may predispose the addict to addiction and those that result from the addiction, lead the addict back to heroin during abstention. Supposedly the addict's inability to handle his life and the demands of society force him into an emotional state that causes him to return to heroin. Our very superficial data seem to support this psychological theory because most of the answers to our simple question hinged upon emotional states.

I am, however, uncomfortable with our findings and the assumption of a psychological theory. We did not go into the circumstances or causes of these emotional states. The addicts may have had good reasons to be in emotional states, and neither our project nor anyone else has pursued the circumstances of these situations. It may very well have been, as Marsh Ray has proposed, something outside the addict, the behavior and attitudes of other persons and society, that caused the relapse rather than his psychological state. This, I believe, has to be considered as a possibility and then ruled out before we can completely accept a psychological theory.

Data supporting the sociological theory of association are just as scarce and shaky as those for a psychological theory. Certainly some addicts relapse after attending treatment when they go back to their old associates, their old haunts. Addict friends and acquaintances are quick to offer the abstainer a taste of their "good dope." Often this seems to be done in a curious kind of self-fulfilling ritual to prove the cliché, "Once an addict always an addict"; it would seem that the friend offers the abstainer drugs to justify his own failure. Returning to addicted associates and the pressures of a community with a high incidence of drug use can cause persons to relapse, but increasingly persons do abstain while continuing to live in a high drug-use area and associating with addicts. This theory may account for some of the high incidence of relapse among urban addicts, but it may be only one of several factors.

More recently, theories of craving and metabolic deficiencies have been postulated to account for relapse. Isidor Chein, after his study of adolescents at Riverside Hospital, postulated a psychophysiological theory of craving to account for the intense drug-seeking behavior of addicts and the tendency to relapse.[10] The idea of craving is a common one, with which we are all familiar—we all crave companionship, love, certain foods, tobacco, and so forth. Addicts use a similar concept to account for their drug-seeking; this is the "yen." This yen, or craving, is an intensive desire that creates within the addict an equally intense emotional reaction and that is only satisfied by the use of an opiate. Substitutes are not accepted. Perhaps the classic example of this craving is revealed in the story of Abraham Wikler about the New York addict who after three years in Lexington Hospital, where he was drug free, started to experience withdrawal-like symptoms the moment he crossed the George Washington Bridge going in to New York. These were so intense he relapsed immediately to heroin, despite an earlier resolve to abstain. Chein, as I have said, developed this theory after completing the study and has not tested it; it remains one of the many unproven theories.

With the development of methadone maintenance Dr. Vincent Dole has taken up the idea of craving, shed its psychological aspects to emphasize the pharmacological, and arrived at a metabolic theory of addiction. In this theory it is postulated that addiicts, after prolonged use of heroin, are subject to some metabolic change or deficiency that creates a drug craving within the individual. As a conse-

10. Isidor Chem *et al., Road to H.*

quence of prolonged use of heroin, addicts experience drug hunger and seek drugs to satisfy a physical need caused by the metabolic deficiency. This deficiency and the associated drug hunger continue long after the addict is withdrawn from heroin and ceases to show withdrawal symptoms.

In some ways this is the most economical theory of relapse we have. If it were in fact proven, it would account for the high incidence and recurrence of relapse in a neat, all-inclusive way. But Dr. Dole does not present any evidence as yet to support his theory; there are presently no known metabolic deficiencies created by heroin use, or by other opiates for that matter. Until some evidence is offered, the theory would seem to be only a pragmatic rationale for the use of methadone maintenance, like the idea of character disorder used by the Synanon-type therapeutic communities, and is no better or worse than the other theories.

It is time that some researcher undertook an in-depth study of relapse that would set out to test all of the theories of relapse— psychological, sociological, pharmacological, and so forth. I specify in-depth, because such a study would have to involve more persons than just the addict. Family members, spouses, lovers, friends and peers, and the program treatment staff should also be involved so that as much as possible could be learned about the individual, his life, his addiction, and the circumstances and reasons for relapse. Such a study would help us to understand more about the phenomenon of relapse.

MOTIVES FOR VOLUNTARY ABSTENTION

I would imagine that the motives for the voluntary abstention reported here are similar to those of persons going into treatment; the hazards of heroin use and the pressures of society force them to abstain. Although we did not ask the specific reasons for the abstentions, most of them were probably the aftermath of some police involvement, incarceration, or prison term. Eddy, whom we discussed earlier, illustrated this in his description of the beginning of his three-year abstention:

> I left New York City to go to Detroit after I left my wife. I just got out of Rikers; did a six month bit for hustling. I had no heroin in the joint, but I started the first day I got out. When I found my wife with this other dude I really busted up. My father was pressuring me to stay off the stuff. My aunt and uncle told me to come to Detroit.

The next day we started back in their car. I took a last shot in their car, threw the works out the window, and kicked that day in my uncle's basement. He gave me a room downstairs and I was sick for three or four days. I guess you can say I was fed up—fed up with going to jail, what had happened with my wife, my whole life.

There was no single reason for Eddie's abstention but a combination of reasons—being in jail, losing his wife, pressure from his family, and feeling that his life was at stake—that led him to take a "geographic cure." Abstention is, I am sure, not possible without some commitment on the user's part. Addicts are quick to tell others that they will not give up drugs unless they want to, and certainly they are right in this respect. The addict has to want to give up heroin before he is able to, but he may find that it is only when he enters some treatment that he changes his mind and decides to give up heroin.

SUMMARY

In summary, it was found that a good number of addicts do abstain from drugs and that for many there are periods of long abstentions. The majority make a reasonable adjustment to society and square life. Usually the abstaining addict works; when he substitutes a drug for heroin it is usually a legal one, alcohol; he gets on with his family and generally avoids the company of other drug users; and he does not engage in hustling or criminal activities. When his family treats him with consideration and refrains from reminding him of his previous addict status, his adjustment is better and he abstains longer.

9

Rock
Bottom

Visible ex-addicts are a relatively new phenomenon; prior to 1965 there were very few ex-addicts who would admit to it.[1] Now and then it would come to public attention that some celebrity, usually a jazz musician, had been addicted and had given it up. Jazz trumpeter Miles Davis was such a man. He was addicted to heroin for a short time early in his musical career and found the strength of character to overcome it. Others who conquered their addictions were Gerry Mulligan, Sonny Rollins, Alexander King, and Bill Stern. Aside from the celebrated, few people admitted that they were ex-addicts—and why should they? The stigma of being an addict was, and perhaps is today, too strong. The addict would be foolish to broadcast his addiction history, for he would suffer as a result.

From time to time there was evidence that there were more addicts who had given up the use of opiates than was known or expected. Charles Winick's study of the Federal Bureau of Narcotics' list of inactive addicts suggested large numbers of ex-addicts.[2] So did

NOTE: Much of the material and many of the ideas in this chapter come from an early working draft by Leon Brill, John Langrod, and George Nash.

1. I have a certain reluctance to use the word *ex-addict*, because as many addicts will tell you (and as I showed in chapter 8), abstention is often short-lived. the term *ex-addict* is certainly an over-simplification, but I use it to avoid sounding too cynical about the future of these men and women.

2. Charles Winick, "Maturing Out of Narcotic Addiction," in *U.N. Bulletin on Narcotics,* Vol. 14 (1962).

Lee Robins' study of a St. Louis school population of black men. He found that 10% of the 235 men reported that they had at one time been addicted to heroin and that at the time of the interview (respondents were 30 to 35 years of age) only 16% of those addicted were still using heroin and 50% were not using heroin but were using other drugs. Furthermore, 14 of the 19 addicts known to the Federal Bureau of Narcotics were considered inactive (not reported for five years) when Robins checked their records. He summarized these findings:

> Whether we accept the figure of 84 percent of heroin addicts free of heroin in the last year, or 74 percent of addicts now inactive by the FBN criterion, it is apparent that heroin addiction has a high remission rate.[3]

Another study, this one a follow-up of former patients at Lexington Hospital, found that while most persons relapsed to drugs within five years after leaving Lexington, large numbers became abstinent. For example, of the 49 white males under 30 years of age who volunteered to enter Lexington Hospital, 73% were using heroin six months after discharge and 8% were abstinent. Five years after discharge the percentage of those voluntarily abstinent rose to 32%, with 34% still using; the remainder were institutionalized or otherwise involuntarily abstinent.[4] With these studies there seemed to be a relatively large number of invisible ex-addicts.

With the new and proliferating treatment programs, namely Synanon and its many off-shoots, various religious programs, and methadone maintenance, there are today many more active and visible ex-addicts. Some, because of employment or involvement with drug treatment programs, are quite willing to let others know and to be frank about their addiction. Frank Natale, the ex-addict codirector of Phoenix Houses, is quite willing to go on television and talk about his addiction to help publicize Phoenix Houses; ex-addicts in various religious programs like Teen Challenge readily admit their "sin as an addict" in testimony to their discovery of God. But most are sensitive to society's stigmatization of addicts and are cooler about their previous history.

Initially our project plan was to follow a known list of addicts, with the hopes of finding some who had given up heroin use on their

3. Lee Robins, "Drug Use in a Normal Population of Young Negro Men," in *American Journal of Public Health*, Vol. 57, no. 9 (1967).

4. Henrietta J. Duval, Ben Z. Locke, and Leon Brill, "Follow-up Study of Narcotic Drug Addicts Five Years after Hospitalization," in *Public Health Reports*, Vol. 78, no. 3 (1963).

own rather than as a consequence of recent treatment experience. This proved to be more difficult and costly than we expected, so the plan was modified to involve study, through in-depth interviews, of some of the processes of deaddiction from a nonrandom sample of persons located mostly through a range of treatment modalities.

Thirty-one addicts were interviewed; 9 by a clinical psychologist, as in-depth case studies, and 20 by a sociologist, with open-ended interview schedules. Two of the addicts took part in both types of interview.

All of the 31 persons were addicts in the true sense; the shortest period of use was 4 years and the longest was 21 years. The median length of use was 9 years. These were by no means experimenters, although there was one who seemed to deny that he had been addicted. A subsequent interview with another addict in the sample who had known the man since childhood corroborated his addiction. According to the second respondent, the first was addicted but did not have to hustle.

Most of those in the sample seemed to fit the stereotypical street addict; that is, they were actively involved in hustling to support their careers. There was, however, one man who attended college during his addiction and completed it when he got off heroin, and a second who made considerable money as a jazz musician and salesman in the garment industry. Both of these were middle-class addicts.

All but four had been arrested and convicted at some time during their heroin careers. At one extreme was a housewife who with her husband had used heroin for 15 years (she snorted for 11 years because she was afraid to use a needle) and who was never arrested because she never bought heroin herself and never had to hustle. At the other extreme was Manuel:

> I have been arrested a total of 16 times, 14 times for drugs and once for murder in the first degree and once for violation of the Sullivan Law. I was cut loose on the murder charge after being held for some time as a suspect.
>
> I was either acquitted or the case dismissed five times. . . . Most of the cases were for acting in concert—that's loitering for the purpose of buying narcotics. . . . In all I did 4 six-month jail terms on Rikers Island, either for possession or works. In 1955 when I was 25 I was sentenced to 5 years in Sing Sing for sales of narcotics. I actually served 37 months.

The majority of the sample had been associated with some drug treatment programs. A third (11) came out of religious programs like the Damascus Church program in New York and Teen Challenge; a second third (10) were in chemotherapy programs (3 in a cyclazocine program and 7 in methadone maintenance). Five were alumni of therapeutic communities (4 from Synanon) and were at the time working in the drug treatment field. The remaining 5 did not cite any particular treatment program as being responsible for their abstentions, though all had been to some program some years before their abstention. This group consisted of addicts who had abstained without the immediate aid of a particular program.

The majority of respondents, 23 out of the 31, were employed in the addiction field; another 3 were seeking work in it. Two of the 4 women were housewives. Three other persons were employed in jobs that were unrelated to the addiction field. The large number of persons working in the addiction field occurred because of the way we solicited interviews; we went to drug programs and asked persons to be interviewed.

All of those we interviewed had been off heroin for at least a year. The median length of time off heroin for the 31 respondents was $3\frac{1}{2}$ years, but two persons had been drug free for ten years—one was an original member of the Damascus Church program and another got off heroin without the aid of any program. None were abusing alcohol or other drugs, but some of the persons in chemotherapy programs reported that they had used heroin on one or two occasions. None felt in danger of returning to heroin use.

The sample is by no means representative of New York addicts or persons in programs, but it was not meant to be. It was selected to explore the processes and events that brought addicts to their decisions to give up heroin. Findings from this study are offered more as impressions than as scientific statements.

PUSHES OUT OF ADDICTION AND ITS ASSOCIATED LIFE

As was discussed in chapter 2, the processes of becoming an addict are rather slow and gradual, with persons using periodically over a long period of time before they become addicted. With this knowledge of gradual addiction it was thought that getting off heroin might also be a gradual process in which the addict cut down on his heroin use over a period of time and gradually gave it up completely. This was not the case; in nearly every instance the men and women studied used heavily up until they joined a program or abstained independently. Heroin use did not dwindle off slowly and gradually fade away. Instead, addicts used heroin full-tilt, and all had strong habits that they terminated abruptly.

This heroin use just before abstention or joining a treatment program nearly always coincided with some crisis or crises in the life of the addict that seemed to push him toward some attempt at abstention or the decision to join a program. These crisis situations were described by some as being a *rock-bottom* period in their addiction careers. Rarely did any two addicts give the same reasons for giving up heroin use, but they all felt that they had reached some low period in their lives where they had to do something about themselves. These rock-bottom crises were in most instances subjective experiences of the individual. For example, the reasons given by the middle-class housewife mentioned earlier, who had if anything a rather easy time of her addiction as compared with most, were the following:

> Right before going into Van Etten Hospital into the cyclazocine program I wrote bad checks, and that really upset me and I decided I had to do something about myself. My habit was costing me about $50 a day, and I knew I couldn't support it. My daughter [adopted daughter] was two and one-half years old and I was taking her to all these different places where the junkies were, and I knew this wasn't any good for her. I couldn't afford to get busted, because who would take care of her.

Objectively, her experiences would seem to arise from quite a different situation from Henry's. He was a black man who had been off heroin ten years when we interviewed him. He gave it up after he reached such a state that addicts ostracized him and would not have anything to do with him:

> After leaving prison at Hart Island he became addicted once more and started to steal from home, pawning his mother's new radio and shoplifting. His mother forced him out of the house, and he started to sleep in cellars, which he had always hated, and developed pustular fungus sores all over his body.
>
> Although he had formerly been very careful and neat about his appearance and bathing, he now no longer cared, went downhill, and did all the things he had previously loathed. He slept in a rat-infested cellar that frequently drained human waste from overflowing toilets down on him. He lived this way for nearly three years, going home on and off, until he became an outcast among junkies, no mean feat. They could not understand how he could live the way he did and described him as disgusting.

Often these rock-bottom situations were violent and caused the addict severe deprivation:

Mercedes, a Puerto Rican woman in her late 30s, said that she decided to give up heroin when she was badly beaten by the police when they arrested her for possession. This beating was so bad that she required hospitalization for a number of weeks. At the time she was also without money, pregnant, and suffering from toxemia.

In most cases addicts reached a low point in their lives where using drugs and life as an addict were intolerable to them, for whatever reason—one rather materialistic man gave up heroin when he realized he had spent his life savings and was going to have to start hustling. The specific set of circumstances is often formed by a complex network of events. The cost of one's habit gets to be too high to manage. It was not uncommon for persons we interviewed to spend as much as $40 or $50 a day for heroin during these periods. It can be difficult to hustle that kind of money every day, and they often experienced severe and recurrent "changes," periods when they did not have enough money to buy heroin, so they did without and suffered withdrawal or substituted whatever they could get at the time.

Hustling became for some too dangerous and distasteful. Addicts, because they find themselves enmeshed in a system of police and courts, are vulnerable to and afraid of arrest. As a habit grows so does the need for hustling, and the more one hustles the greater chances of getting caught. Getting arrested meant the certainty of withdrawal sickness (less now than when we were interviewing because persons are often withdrawn in New York jails now), with a period of time in jail awaiting a court trial and a possible prison term upon conviction. Many said that they just got tired of the round of stealing, dealing, and robberies that they continually had to resort to. They disliked what they had to do to get heroin and said that the more they fit the "street junkie" image, the more uncomfortable they felt.

Still others felt that they were tired of continually going to jail and prisons, of suffering the degradation and dehumanization that are part and parcel of incarceration. One woman in her late 20s joined Synanon to get out of the Nevada State Prison, where she had been sent with a 10- to 20-year sentence for sales of marijuana and possession of heroin:

> I got tired of taking drugs, because I kept going to jail, but I didn't think I would ever get out of it even by joining Synanon. I surprised myself and did.

Heroin use becomes too much trouble and the addict reaches a saturation level where all the negative aspects of heroin use and

the "life" outweigh whatever positive things he got from the drug.
The life is no longer exciting, but intolerable. The hazards get him
down so he makes some commitment to give up heroin. There may,
most certainly, be other societal pressures or circumstances involved
—going to jail, being put on probation or parole, and so forth—but
the individual must decide to give up drugs before these have any
real effect upon his behavior, and rock bottom usually forces that
decision.

It would seem that the addict simply "burns out," gives up his
defenses for his use of heroin and acquiesces to society's pressures.
He no longer can bear society's disdain, the stigma of the addict, the
things he must do to get drugs, the ways the police treat him, the
demeaning nature of jails and prisons, the continual "changes" he
must go through to use drugs. Society has gotten the advantage over
him and, like poet-playwright Bertolt Brecht's peasant in his peasant's philosophy toward authority, he does not say "no" as he has in
the past but "yes"—because he knows that society has the upper
hand and what can it do when it stands over you. He says "yes" to
life; he might want to continue to use drugs but he realizes it is
too much trouble. These are the pushes of protracted heroin use and
the addict's life, but there are also some pulls, some attractions to
lure the addict away from heroin use.

PULLS INTO THE SQUARE LIFE

As the life of the street gets harsh and difficult, as one has to
give up more and more just to satisfy the need for drugs, as one has
to go to jail more and more often, so does the mundane, predictable
life of the square, with its comforts and possessions, begin to appeal
to the addict. No longer is the life of the square disdained as being
dull and uninteresting. Now it is seen as being "normal," easy, and
comfortable—something to long for. One man told us, pure and
simple:

> I stopped using drugs because I wanted everything from life—a car,
> a decent apartment, and a family. I'm very materialistic and you can't
> have anything while you are a dope fiend.

It seems that when the possibility of acquiring the "good life" is cut
off by the use of heroin, the square life and its values become more
attractive to the addict; they become something to dream about, to
long for, and to try to attain.

It is not particularly difficult to comprehend the increased attractiveness of square life when the possibility of achieving it becomes remote. The addict knows from his own experience that you do not quite appreciate what you have until you lose it. Freedom to move about and do what you want means little while you have it; it means a good deal more when you go to jail or prison and it is denied you. Square life is easy to disdain or take for granted while you have a chance to live it, but when you lose that chance it begins to look much more attractive than it ever did before.

The major value system of the United States—despite the many assaults by the contemporary youth culture—emphasizes work, stable family life, and a certain level of consumption. Addicts, though they may talk out against these values, are not immune to them. These things are attractive to the addict, more so when they seem remote or out of reach, and they become goals for him as they are for the square.

THE ROLE OF OTHERS

Sociological studies have shown that others—parents, spouses, relatives, teachers—play an important part in helping persons to select a life work and, when that life work is over, to endure an often lonely and impoverished old age. Parents, relatives, and teachers—as they serve as role models—are crucial in helping young persons to select occupations. Daughters, sons, and relatives are important in sustaining old people who might otherwise become ill and depressed upon the death of a spouse. Aging men who somehow lack these familial relationships in old age become cut off from society and have the highest suicide rate of any age group in the United States.

It seemed natural to ask what role, if any, other persons played in the efforts of addicts to abstain from heroin. Only 2 out of the 31 interviewed cited relatives, spouses, or friends as being important in helping them get over their addiction. One man's mother stuck by him through eight years of addiction:

When he came back from his last stay in jail he found his mother's apartment closed and became very afraid that she had died while he was in jail. Inquiring from neighbors, he learned that she had been ill and staying with his sister. He went to the sister's house, expecting to be turned away because of the callous ways he had used both of them but was surprised when they both met him kindly and took him in once again. He knew then he would never use drugs again, since he had had all he could take and felt reassured by the fact that his mother and sister had accepted him.

Another Puerto Rican man went to a friend and told him of a wild and foolish plan to rob a bank:

> I had decided that I was going to have money or get killed doing it. I got a hold of an old hand grenade and prepared a note telling the teller to give me $5,000 or else. I went to Manuel, an old friend, and told him the plan. He looked at me strange, tore up the note, and said, "You must be sick and need help." He then did a strange thing; he went and sold his overcoat, in the middle of winter, and gave me the money to buy drugs to get straight. This is something that I will never forget. When things were so bad for me he was still my friend.

These were the only instances where friends or family were reported to have any strong, positive influence over the addict's life. The reasons are obvious. Addicts, over the long course of their addiction, tend to exhaust their social credit with friends and relatives and to destroy relationships that might be of some future help to them. Often they repeatedly steal and borrow from both family and friends; after a time the victims cannot tolerate them anymore and cut them loose. They "burn their bridges" with their families and friends.

Then again, many never have particularly good relationships to begin with. Often relations with parents are poor or destructive to begin with and tend to contribute to the individual's addiction, so they would be little help to him to overcome it. These are men and women who for some reason could not establish and maintain long, satisfying relationships with other people.

If family, relatives, and friends were of little or no direct help to the group of addicts, persons in treatment facilities *were* important and helpful to them. Generally these persons were leaders or high-ranking staff members in programs who became for the addicts symbols of care and concern. Addicts we interviewed from religious programs cited ministers as giving them inspiration to accept God and the church community; others cited Drs. Marie Nyswander and Joyce Lowenson, leaders of the methadone maintenance programs, and Charlie Dederich of Synanon. In some ways relationships with program leaders served as substitutes for the personal relationships that the addict had previously been unable to attain or had destroyed. In a sense their attachments to drug treatment programs are similar to their associations with drug users when they first began to use heroin.

In the effort to overcome addiction the addict often tries to forge a new identity, different from the addict-dope fiend, in a new community. Successful programs for the addict offer both—a new identity and a different community. This is most apparent in religious programs. Those who overcome their addiction through religious orientations accept the idea that they have been sinful and have misbehaved as an addict in defiance of God. As one Puerto Rican man who had been in the Damascus Church program explained:

> The body is God's Temple and it should not be defiled. Even smoking and drinking can defile the body.

They become sinners who are saved by giving themselves to God. In turn, they are accepted wholeheartedly in the church community and work actively to help others with similar problems. Some even become ministers themselves or are working toward it.

In therapeutic communities (in most instances Synanon) the participants find not only charismatic leaders to identify with but a number of addicts like themselves who express friendship by caring for them in new and unexpected ways. This friendship may take the form of severe and active criticism of their behavior, but in the context of the community this is accepted and expected as good and responsible behavior on the part of active members. In this way some of the very same people (or persons like them) with whom they used drugs and hustled come to help them overcome just these behaviors. This is exemplified in the statement of Isidor, a Jew in his late 30s, who said that his whole Synanon tribe helped him get over drugs:

> I liked it when I could express all the anger and hate I felt and they weren't punitive. It was nothing like all those other institutions (Riverside, Lexington, Manhattan State, etc.) I had been in.

Drug treatment programs, their leaders and staff, program ideologies, and their efficacy all serve as attractions to addicts. Each program has its own street reputation, which may often be different from other public reputations. Addicts who go into some treatment and manage to abstain and demonstrate a new or changed life are to the addict population the best advertisement of a program. They attract other addicts to the program because they are seen to be "clean" and looking good.

TRUE BELIEVERS

Ideologies are emphasized strongly in drug treatment programs. More often than not the person who comes out of a treatment program incorporates the ideology of his particular program into his personal philosophy and rejects *all* other program ideologies. Synanon residents are particularly vociferous in this regard. They become converted to Synanon and actively proselytize for the program, often to the point of seeming rigid and denying the obvious.

While the acceptance of an ideology may not be acceptable in a social scientist studying drug programs, it is, I believe, understandable in the case of the successfully treated addict. Drug theories and ideologies—those that say the addict has a character disorder, is a sinner, is a victim of a metabolic deficiency—may appear to the outsider as too simplistic and unrealistic, but they are often important organizing principles for a person attempting to overcome addiction and make a new life for himself. An ideology gives the ex-addict a framework within which to understand and interpret his past behavior—he was a sinner, childish, a victim of his environment; it helps temper whatever guilt or remorse he may feel for undoubtably many antisocial acts; and it provides him with rough guidelines for how to live in the future. It becomes a philosophy of life.

For example, methadone patients often expressed the idea that addiction could happen to anyone, particularly to persons who lived in impoverished ghettoes, where drugs were all around them. They believed this because their program did not specify that any particular psychological or moral condition was responsible for heroin use and addiction but rather that the individual had gotten caught up in an inappropriate life style that prescribed heroin use and that after using it for some time he found that he could not stop. No intensive soul-searching or confession were required, as is the case with therapeutic communities and religious programs, but the addict was expected to apply himself to changing his life style. The methadone program emphasized a responsible life and steady work and exerted active and strong pressure upon patients to conform to society's norms. These goals are not unlike those of Synanon and religious programs; perhaps the differences between the programs are not as great as one has been led to expect. The differences occur in how these goals are attained. The methadone program does not operate on a psychological theory of addiction; it does not require patients to explore their motivations or behavior.

LONG-TERM EFFECTS OF TREATMENT

The effectiveness of drug treatment programs was not always immediately apparent for our sample of persons. Often they relapsed after a stay in treatment but later, in retrospect, said that the program had been important in their efforts to get off heroin. All five of the persons who did not cite particular drug programs as being responsible for their getting off heroin had been to some treatment and relapsed after that stay but had still gotten something from it:

> Juan, a Puerto Rican in his late 20s at the time of the interview, had been in Riverside Hospital in 1960 but continued to use heroin for five more years after he left. He stopped using drugs more or less on his own, but this is how he remembered Riverside Hospital: "When I first went in I was mad at the world. I left after 34 days; I came back though and being in the hospital really helped. The person who helped me the most was my therapist at Riverside, who I saw in 1960. She socked reality to me when I was a kid. She was very helpful. She told me the truth, which I denied. Even though I rebelled against what she told me, later on when I was in prison I thought about her a lot.

It was not just the staffs of the programs that had an impact upon the addict, as is evident in the description of the various treatment experiences of Jesus:

> I went to Lexington, Ky., no less than seven times and also attempted withdrawal at East Harlem Protestant Parish, Central Islip, Manhattan State, Morris Bernstein, Metropolitan, and Riverside Hospital. Oh, I made all the places, but I couldn't make it in any of them. I even began private therapy with Dr. Nyswander in 1958; did that for 7 months.

> Then I went to Psychiatric Institute and was in an experiment that let dope fiends use drugs to see if they could regulate it themselves and get off. Well, there were so many crazies, psychotics, around there, I was too upset by the place to withdraw myself. Well, while I was there I saw, I saw myself, how these crazy, sick people changed sometimes in a very short time, like over a week or a few days. I knew then that people could change; those way-out patients could change, so I knew I could.

There were other events and issues in Jesus's addict career that pushed him out of drugs, but this experience showed him that "human nature" was changeable and that he might change also.

156

CAREERS IN DOPE

Undoubtedly when addicts reach rock bottom and go into treatment the treatment plays a major role in helping them to overcome heroin use. But not every institutionalization insures abstention or rehabilitation by any means. Many addicts have long histories of jail and treatment experience. Some actually develop an institutional life style in which they spend most of their time in jails or treatment. One 32-year-old man whom I interviewed at Phoenix House had spent 22 of his 32 years in institutions—an orphanage, two reform schools, innumerable jails and treatment programs—and made only occasional forays into the outside world when he used heroin for a short time and then went back "home" to jail or treatment. He had adapted to institutionalization very well and said he was quite comfortable. All of his needs were cared for, the regime was predictable, and he was always on his good behavior so he got out of the joint after a short stay. His joint was not unlike the *Joint* of another addict, James Blake, who in his book of the same name described his own amniotic environment:

> . . . it is in every moment and every action part of my life. I think always of the peace that I had there—this working to survive and surviving to work seems increasingly like an arrangement I would not have chosen were it up to me. [Blake wrote this during one of his short stays outside of prison.] Those gates, man, they're inviting. So much lovely time stretches out before you, time to read, to write, to play, to practice, to speculate, contemplate—and without the idiot necessity to Hold Up Your End . . . it is infinitely restful.[5]

There are most definitely a lot of ways to adapt to the world and some addicts actually enjoy institutionalization, as grizzly as that may seem. But even for those who do not feel the pull of institutions, after treatment or incarceration abstention is a difficult and often tenuous achievement.

Addicts may be repulsed by their lives and may get what is considered help in treatment or in some institution yet still be unable to resist heroin. There are, to say the least, powerful forces that keep the addict enmeshed in heroin use and its associated life. For some it may be the very reasons they became addicted—some unresolved need for a release of tension or anxiety; some need for an identity, a community, or a vocation—that keep them in the system. Then along the course of their addiction they pick up some additional statuses and stigma to live up to or overcome—they become thieves or ex-convicts.

5. See James Blake's letters to Nelson Algren and James Purdy in his book *The Joint* (New York: Doubleday & Company, Inc., 1971).

The fact that an addict is known to the authorities and the establishment as a drug user can block his attempts to abstain and live a different life. He may be unable to get a driver's license or to be bonded; he may find that certain jobs (usually high-paying and civil-service jobs) are barred to him. He may not be able to get a job or manage his life during those first important weeks after he returns to the outside world. He may have no alternative but to live in a high-drug-use area, where he is surrounded by drug users and the temptations of heroin that he is trying to overcome. These factors combine to make abstention a difficult task. The addict may "burn out" or go into treatment to overcome his addiction but still be unable to abstain from heroin or change his life because there are so many forces that mitigate against his resolve to give up heroin and against whatever help he may have received. The point is that there may be not one but several rock bottoms for the addict to face.

THE RIGHT COMBINATIONS

Up to now I have talked as if the pushes and pulls on an addict trying to overcome his addiction were independent and isolated; they are, rather, interdependent and there are relationships between the experiences of rock-bottom crises, the attractions of square life, and, for those who took that route, treatment programs. As an addict's life becomes too difficult, too dysfunctional, square life becomes a preferred alternative. Most treatment programs offer the "good life," the square alternative, through living examples—the ex-addict staff members.

Sometimes the combination of pushes, pulls, and treatment is fortuitous. For example, one Puerto Rican man we interviewed, José, met Reverend Rosado, founder of the Damascus Church Narcotics Crusade program, while he was in jail, and he became one of the core group of that program. Reverend Rosado, a fundamentalist minister, was looking for addicts to start a program, and José was at wit's end. The minister offered José a "new life," or the prospect of a new life, and while José was not particularly religious at the time he had no other viable alternative. He joined the program upon release from jail—he had promised the judge to join—and became actively involved in the Christian life of the program. It obviously provided him with whatever it was he needed to help him embark upon a new life, because when we interviewed him he had been abstinent for 10 years, was actively involved in his church community, and was directing a similar religious program for addicts.

More often the right combination would seem to be one of rock bottom and the offerings of treatment programs. Addicts know about treatment programs, from either their own or other's experiences, and they may be selective about joining programs. Right combinations are important in drug treatment because there are at once a wide range of programs and, with only one exception, methadone maintenance, only a moderate or low rate of success.

The correct combination of rock bottom and treatment has to emerge before the addict can utilize a program to best advantage. Put another way, the addict has to make a genuine commitment to change his life, and the program has to be one that is right for him, one that appeals to him or otherwise convinces him that it can change his life. The right combination, sometimes even many years after, gives the individual what he needs—a new faith, a new attitude, a physical support, a new model for life—to help him give up heroin use and its associated life. The growing numbers of visible ex-addicts belie that cynical old saw, *once an addict always an addict.*

[10]

Women
Versus Men

In the often variable statistics on the numbers of addicts presented by the treatment programs of Federal and State agencies, male addicts are said to outnumber female addicts by as much as 9 to 1. This ratio varies considerably; during 1968 at the California Rehabilitation Center, the largest narcotic treatment facility in California, males outnumbered females 6 to 1; at Synanon, a private, self-help therapeutic community in Santa Monica, California, the ratio declines to 2 to 1. In the same year at the facilities of the New York State Narcotics Addiction Control Commission there were 9 males to every female, but this declines to 4.5 to 1 in the New York City Phoenix Houses. At the Federal Hospital in Lexington, Kentucky, in 1965 the ratio was 6 to 1. Still another ratio of males to females is that published by the United States Bureau of Narcotics during 1967; their cumulative registry of active narcotics addicts in the United States shows a ratio of 5 to 1. Further complicating the picture, the New York City Registry of drug abusers, which has registered all known drug abusers in New York City from a variety of sources—police arrest records, hospital detoxification units, public and private narcotic treatment facilities—reports that there are 4 men to every woman among the 100,000 drug abusers registered between 1964 and 1969. This last is probably the best estimate, because it comes from a variety of sources.

Whatever the exact ratio of men to women, the predominance

of male over female addicts has caused female addicts to be nearly completely neglected by researchers in the field. The literature on women addicts is very sparse compared to the reams produced each year that deal with men; as in other areas, researchers have overlooked the special problems of women addicts and have been content to generalize from the data about men. Isidor Chein *et al.* in their book *The Road to H* devoted only a short chapter to women; the sample was small, only 20 persons. There is an occasional journal article, with the best of these coming out of Lexington Hospital.[1] In commercial literature there are several brief but illuminating descriptive life histories in a book entitled *The Junkie Priest,* the story of Father Egan, S.A., as told to John D. Harris. The best thing about women is a compelling and brilliantly told autobiography recorded by Howard Becker and edited by Helen Hughes. This is *The Fantastic Lodge,* which in my estimation is the finest book of its kind written about heroin use. Fortunately it was recently reissued by Fawcett Publications and is again available.

IMPRESSIONS ABOUT WOMEN

Talking to male addicts and to persons who work in treatment facilities for women, one hears continually that female addicts are different from male addicts. They are said to use more drugs, to be more often deviant sexually, and to be generally more emotional and less stable than their male counterparts. In the words of each, the male addict and the persons who attempt to rehabilitate them, women addicts are said to be more often "fucked up" and "sicker."

Many male addicts claim that female addicts are not to be trusted, are without scruples, and will stoop to anything to get the drugs that they need. Undoubtedly a good deal of the male addict's attitudes and criticisms of the female come from first-hand experience—women are nearly always "turned on" to heroin by a male, quite often by boy friends, lovers, and husbands, and when they almost inevitably turn to the street and to prostitution to seek money for drugs, it is the male addict who has instigated and encouraged that professionalization. Indeed, much of this rancor of the male addict comes from some well of guilt about his own relationships with female addicts.

Persons who attempt to treat and rehabilitate women addicts

1. See Chambers et al. (1968, 1970), Pescor (1944), Ellinwood et al. (1966), and Glaser (1966) in the bibliography.

in several programs say that they act out, are overly emotional, are defensive of their drug use, form homosexual relationships within the treatment facilities easily, "game less," and respond to treatment more.

In our own experience the women addicts that we talked with in two different treatment facilities were initially much more difficult to interview than men—the interview relationship was harder to establish, many were indifferent to the situation, some were actually hostile to it, it was harder to establish rapport, and it was harder to make the situation a pleasant experience. On the other hand, some of our best, most productive in-depth interviews were with these same women, and when care was taken to match interviewer to interviewee according to sex (men interviewed more feminine-appearing women addicts and females interviewed those appearing less feminine) many of the problems encountered earlier were overcome. The summary of our impressions was that women seemed to show many more problems relating to people (or specifically, prying, middle-class interviewers) and are openly contemptuous of situations that male addicts handle with greater ease and less contempt.

What, if any, are the specific differences between men and women addicts aside from the obvious sex and role differences? This is the subject of this chapter, which draws upon data from a survey of 122 women addicts conducted over the course of two years at the Manhattan Rehabilitation Center and 226 men in four NACC facilities—Bayview, Edgecombe, Woodbourne, and Manhattan State. The 122 women in the sample were interviewed at two different times. The first stratified, random sample was taken during August and September of 1968 and consisted of 70 persons. The second one, which was part of a larger study to determine the changes over time at the treatment facility, was made during August of 1968 and consisted of 52 women. All of the 226 men were interviewed at one sampling during August and September of 1968.[2]

The mean age for both groups, male and female, was 24 years. The mean length of heroin use was five years, with a range of from one month to 32 years. Blacks were represented more often in both samples than were whites and Puerto Ricans. Somewhat more of the females were black than the males (50% of the females and 42% of the males).

Both groups came from working-class families, as indicated by

2. This is only part of a larger sample of 422 men; men from Phoenix Houses are excluded from this analysis.

the job of the head of the household and the education of the father. More than 3 out of 4 of the heads of the households were in skilled, semiskilled, or unskilled occupations.

The major religious group in our sample was Catholic; more than half (55%) were raised in that religion, two out of five (39%) were Protestant, and only a small number (3%) were Jewish, the major religious and ethnic group in New York City.

FAMILY DISORGANIZATION

The principal differences between the male and female heroin addicts in our samples were in the disorganization of family life, certain economic insecurity, the presence of addiction and alcoholism within the family, sexual deviance, criminality before heroin use, and use of treatment facilities.

Despite the general overemphasis by Freudian psychologists and psychiatrists on the effects of family life on individuals' subsequent personalities and on their social adjustment, and despite the more current antithetical and existential treatment belief that an unhappy family life should not be a rationalization for antisocial or destructive behavior, the experience of a family and particularly its dissolution or breakdown has a strong effect upon a person's subsequent life—the way that he views himself, the kind of adjustment that he makes, the way he raises his children, and so forth. The experience of growing up in a broken family stays with most of those who suffer it. Even if the effect is to compensate for or to create the reverse of the family experience, it has left its mark. The impact of family disorganization on children is summarized rather concisely by William J. Goode in his article "Family Disorganization" (1961):

It is difficult to measure exactly the impact of family disorganization upon children. Without question, children are more likely to grow up to be law-abiding, healthy, and happy adults if they spent their entire childhood in a happy family than they are if the family unit is broken by divorce or death. . . .

The general association of broken homes with delinquency has been demonstrated by many studies. . . . Even when the class position is held constant, the delinquency rate of children is higher for broken than for unbroken homes. Similarly, the rate of delinquency among boys and girls is higher for those whose parents are separated or divorced than it is for those who lost a parent by death.

Unfortunately, for those who seek easy solutions of family disorganization, it almost seems likely that a family in which there is a continual marital conflict, or separation, is more likely to produce children of personal adjustment than a family in which there is a divorce or death. . . . The evidence so far suggests that it is the conflict of divorce, not the divorce itself, that has an impact upon children.[3]

In order to learn something of family disorganization we asked each of the addicts in our samples:

Who did you live with when you were five years old, ten years old, fifteen years old, twenty years old?

Only 1 in 3 (34%) of the women reported that they had lived with both parents through their fifteenth year, while almost half (46%) of the men reported living with both mother and father until they were 15 years old. By far the majority of women (66%) grew up in homes that were broken by divorce, separation, or death, while considerably fewer (54%) of the males experienced such disorganization. Furthermore, 6% of the males and 13% of the females reported that they had not at any of these ages lived with both parents.

It was more often the father who was absent from the home —2 out of every 5 (40%) of the females reported that they had not lived either with a father or a stepfather when they were five, ten, fifteen, or twenty years of age. An additional 13% reported that they had not lived with their mothers at any of these ages, and a still larger number, 23%, reported that they had lived only with their mothers when they were five or ten.

The extent of family disorganization is illustrated by the family histories of Beverly and Marie:

> Beverly is a slim, attractive, 22-year-old Caucasian who began the use of opiates (dilaudid) when she was 17 years old and used on and off for four years before she was apprehended for stealing and was allowed to choose a civil certification in the state program. She described her family as follows:
>
>> My father drank and my mother cheated; she always had a lot of boy friends. They were always at each other ever since I can remember. We had a dreadful thing. They couldn't manage any of us—never could. One day when I was 11 years old my mother threw my father and my two brothers out of the house. They went down the street to my grandmother's house and I stayed with her a month and then I went to join my father when I was getting in her way. I went back and forth between the both of them so much I never knew where I was. Living with both of them was pretty dreadful. He couldn't control us—we did what-

3. William J. Goode, "Family Disorganization," in *Contemporary Social Problems* (ed. Robert K. Merton and Robert A. Nisbet. New York: Harcourt Brace Jovanovich, Inc., 1961).

ever we wanted; she was always too strict and too busy with her boy friends to care about any of us.

Marie is a pretty, 24-year-old Puerto Rican woman who used heroin for 21 months prior to her commitment to Manhattan Rehabilitation Center in 1967 and then for another 13 months while on aftercare. Marie did not know her real father until she was nine. He and her mother were divorced when Marie was three years old, but when she was nine she and her mother visited him a few times in the Bronx. Her mother married again when she was five, and that ended when it was discovered that the man was a bigamist. Again her mother married; this time when she was 12. This marriage ended when it was discovered that the man did not own a business as he claimed and in fact never worked at all during the marrage. Marie had little to do with any of these "husbands" and she got along with the last only through an arrangement they had where she wouldn't tell her mother that he didn't go to work and he wouldn't tell the mother of her beginning use of barbiturates and amphetamines. By the time she was 14 Marie was skipping school a great deal because of her drug use and then was placed in a "Catholic home," where she remained until she was 17. Marie never really knew a father and her only pleasurable memories of a father are those few visits to the Bronx when her real father took her and her mother shopping, to dinner, and to the movies.

Ethnicity is associated with family disorganization; more black and Puerto Rican than white women from our sample came from disrupted homes. Only 3 out of 10 blacks and Puerto Ricans (respectively 29% and 31%) reported that they had lived with their mothers and fathers through their fifteenth years, while over half of the whites did (52%). Of the three groups, blacks and Puerto Ricans suffered more family disorganization than whites. This pattern of black and Puerto Rican family disorganization is as one would expect; both are deprived minority groups in New York.

Another item of data that indicated the instability of the family life of women addicts was the degree to which they were compatible with their families before their heroin use. We asked both men and women:

> In general, how well did you get along with your family and other relatives before you used heroin?

One quarter (25%) of the 120 women who answered this question said they got along poorly, or at times poorly and at times well, while only 1 in 10 (11%) of the 218 men gave this answer. Moreover, more than 3 out of 5 of the men (61%) said they got along very well with their family and relatives, while only 46% of the women reported getting along very well.

Traditionally, family members generally exert much more control, social and physical, over females than over males. Men are allowed much more freedom to roam—to experiment sexually, to express themselves as individuals, and so forth—than women are. Women are kept close to home for fear of pregnancy, to assure physical protection, and because much more of the activity of their future role as mother and housekeeper, as well as other roles they may play, are centered in the home. It seems to me that where there is friction in the home among any of its members girls would be much more sensitive to it because of their intense and constant association with family members. Boys, on the other hand, are free to seek more and diverse relationships, so they are less liable to invest as much emotion as girls.

Again ethnicity is associated with family compatibility. White females report less family compatibility than either blacks or Puerto Ricans. More than 2 out of every 5 (44%) of our white females reported getting along with their families either poorly or at times poorly and at times well, while only 1 in 5 of both the blacks (20%) and Puerto Ricans (21%) said this. Correspondingly, half of the blacks (52%) and Puerto Ricans (50%) reported that they got along very well with their families before heroin use, while less than a quarter (24%) of the whites could report such compatibility.

This difference among ethnic groups may be accounted for by the variation in degrees of social control the various ethnic groups exert upon their female members. Working-class blacks generally give more freedom to females than do whites, and this may account for some differences between the two races. It does not, however, account for the large differences between whites and Puerto Ricans, which I am at a loss to explain.

Addiction and Alcoholism in the Family

This general disorganization in the families of women addicts is further compounded by a relatively high incidence of both heroin addiction and alcoholism within the families. If, as many have claimed, narcotic addiction is contagious, then the presence of addiction within the family itself may result in the addiction of other members of that family. Heroin use and addiction do not occur in a social vacuum, but within a definite social and cultural milieu, as we saw in chapter 2. It doesn't take a necessarily inordinate curiosity for a person to experiment with heroin and then to become addicted.

In an effort to learn something of the association between the individual's heroin addiction and heroin addiction and alcoholism within the family, our interviewers asked all the men and women in our sample two questions having to do with drugs and the family. In the response to the first question:

Were any of the relatives you ever lived with addicted to heroin?

1 in 5 (20%) of the females reported that they had lived with a relative who was addicted to heroin, while only 1 in 10 of the men (10%) reported living with an addicted relative. Both males and females cited siblings more often than parents or other relatives. Male addicts usually reported an addicted brother, while female addicts reported a sister. One woman reported a twin being addicted; another reported a sister and five brothers addicted. One of the men we spoke to at Bayview (but did not interview formally) reported that his whole family was addicted—mother, stepfather, and three brothers. His mother was one of the women in the time-two sample of 52.

The second question relating to drug abuse in the family asked:

Did any of the relatives you lived with have a problem with drinking?

Again, women reported a higher incidence than did men; 31% of the women reported that they lived with a relative with a drinking problem, while 21% of the men reported such a problem. Quite different from addiction in the family, alcoholism ("problems with drinking") was generally the behavior of parents rather than siblings for both male and female groups.

When I combined the answers to the two questions about heroin addiction and alcohol problems, it was found that nearly half (46%) of the women in our samples had lived in families where one of the members was either a heroin addict or had problems with drinking, while only a little over a quarter (26%) of the men reported such addiction or alcoholism. Drug problems in the families of women were much more prevalent than they were with men and probably compounded the general family disorganization suffered by the majority of the women.

Of the two problems, addiction and alcoholism, the alcoholism of a parent or parents would appear to be much more destructive than the addiction of a sibling, simply because children are much more dependent upon their parents for sustenance than they are upon siblings. Even in instances where there was considerable sibling rivalry, the addiction of a sibling might have little or no effect on other children because they could use the addiction of a brother or sister as an opportunity to show more favorably in the eyes of the parent.

Women also tend more to have lived with an addicted spouse or lover than men do. When we asked respondents if the last spouse or lover they lived with was addicted, more than half (54%) of the women who had lived with a husband or lover reported "yes," while less than one in five (19%) of the men had. This, I believe, is one of the most important differences between men and women addicts.

Men, for a number of reasons, tend *not* to live with addicted women. The first reason is that men usually become addicted at an earlier age and as a consequence are more apt to remain single or unattached. Male addicts considerably outnumber female addicts (perhaps 4 to 1) and there obviously are not enough women addicts to go around even if we do not count those who live with other women or otherwise do not become attached to men. In addition to these reasons are the working-class male's conception of marriageable women, which in most instances rules out addicted women, and most men's double moral standard.

Women, on the other hand, reported living with an addicted spouse or lover more often, because they are frequently turned on to heroin by a spouse or lover and because—in what appears to be a recurring pattern—in the early stages of their careers in addiction they often live with the more competent or resourceful addicts, who are either good thieves or relatively successful drug sellers and who supply them with drugs and otherwise support them.

Marriage or love between two addicts appears to compound their problems. A single addiction is expensive enough; two within a single family would stretch the resources of all but the wealthy or the best hustlers. Supporting his own addiction is often more than most males can manage; supporting two, unless the male is particularly competent, is something that only women are capable of. This seems to reverse the economic relationship of men and women that is usually seen in the United States. In this relationship men become less competent than women to sustain the economy of the couple or family. This may cause considerable friction between the two and perhaps undermine the male's feelings of competence.

Love and marriage among addicts seem to be strongest while one or the other is in jail, in some residential treatment, or recently released. Love is a tenuous and fragile state while one or the other is using heavily or "strung out." The need for drugs is so strong during these periods that it is very difficult to consider another person except as they aid or impede satisfaction.

The incarceration or residential treatment of one or both of the partners seems to intensify the feelings of the one incarcerated or in treatment. During these periods the addict has a good deal of time to mull over past relationships, to relive the past and dream about the future. At the same time he or she may start to have a resurge in sexual drive and to feel a strong sexual need. It is during these periods that love blossoms among addicts—letters are written and grand plans are made for an eventual release.

OTHER STUDIES

How do these findings compare with other studies? In terms of family disorganization there is agreement with some research[4] and disagreement with others.[5] In those studies where there is disagreement, there was considerable variation in the ethnicity of the sample.[6] Furthermore, research in Lexington Hospital suggests that there are geographic differences among addicts—most particularly between those from the South and those from the Northeast, between big-city addicts and rural or small-town addicts. All of our addicts were from New York State, and only a very few lived outside of New York City. This would suggest that any generalization of our findings should be limited to big-city addicts or to New York City addicts. It should, however, be remembered that as of 1969 there were 95,000 known narcotic abusers in New York City, and some persons estimate that as high as 55% of all of the addicts in the United States reside in New York City.

The data on addiction and alcoholism in the family agree with one study and disagree with another, but these differences may also be for geographic reasons.[7]

FINANCIAL INSECURITY

Ever since World War II the great incidence of addiction in America has been concentrated in the slums and ghettoes of our largest cities. Within large cities, addiction in the United States does

4. The data agreed with Pescor (1944), Chein (1964), Hall (1938), and Chambers et al. (1970) (see the bibliography).

5. The disagreement is with Chambers et al. (1968) and Ellinwood et al. (1966) (see the bibliography).

6. Chambers' sample was all black and Ellinwood's was 60% white.

7. Agreement was with Pescor (1944), and disagreement with Ellinwood et al (1966).

not necessarily cut across class or socioeconomic lines. Despite the recent awareness of the increase in addiction in middle-class suburban communities, the bulk of heroin addicts come from the mass of poor and disenfranchised persons who live in deteriorating slums and ghettoes and who suffer the original sin of Kurt Weill's and Bertolt Brecht's opera *Mahagonny*—"they have no money."

Financial instability and poverty also figure in the story of the female addict's family. More women (35%) than men (25%) said "yes" to this question:

Was your family ever on welfare when you were growing up?

In many ways, family stability in our culture is dependent upon a certain degree of financial independence. The stigma and degradation felt by persons applying for and receiving welfare is well known; the effect is often to shake the strength of the family. This is to say nothing of general welfare policies that permit welfare assistance to be withheld or stopped when a man who is thought to be capable of work is living in a household. It has been these policies, as well as a history of slavery, that have decimated many black families.

Ethnic differences among those reporting financial instability are dramatic. More than 2 out of every 5 (46%) of the Puerto Rican women and one-third (37%) of black women reported that their families had been on welfare at some point when they were growing up. The differences between these two groups and the white women were, respectively, 29% and 20%; only 1 in 6 of the white women in our sample (17%) reported having been on welfare while they were growing up. The high incidence of financial instability in the Puerto Rican group as opposed to the black group was unexpected. We had thought that—given the long history of slavery, the disorganization of the black family, and the general bars to blacks of employment opportunities—the incidence of blacks reporting being on welfare would be higher than the other two groups. This disadvantage of the Puerto Ricans may be the result of their more recent migration and of resultant problems with the English language.

CRIMINALITY

Crime statistics indicate that in general women commit fewer criminal acts than do men. Addiction seems to equalize the sexes in this regard. When we asked both men and women about certain hustles (using the list mentioned earlier in chapter 3), we found that there was no difference between men and women in terms of acts *ever* committed; there was, however, considerable difference between self-reported criminal activities before heroin use. Nearly 4 out of 5 (79%) of the women we interviewed reported that they had *not* committed any of the acts on the list prior to heroin use, while only slightly more than half (55%) of the men reported *no* criminality before heroin use. This is, however, what one would expect.

What was unexpected were the surprising differences among race and ethnic groups in our sample. One would expect that white women who came from more financially stable families and who suffered less family disorganization would be less likely to commit criminal acts before heroin use; however, this is not the case. Both Puerto Rican and black women in our sample reported much less criminal activity before heroin use than white women of our sample did. Only 1 in 10 (8%) of Puerto Rican women and 2 in 10 (18%) of the black women report committing some of the acts listed above, as compared to nearly one half (48%) of the white women.

Interpreted in the light of the Anslinger-Lindesmith theories about addicts being criminal or not criminal before their heroin use, our data would indicate that white female addicts before their heroin use are much more criminal as a group than both their black and Puerto Rican counterparts.

A similar difference holds for the younger persons in our sample. Fewer of those over 26 years of age reported that they had committed criminal activities before heroin use than did those under 26. Only 1 in 10 (10%) of those over 26 years of age reported some previous criminal activity, while more than one-quarter (27%) of those from 21 to 26 years of age, and nearly the same proportion (23%) of those under 21, reported committing one or more of the activities listed. It would appear that women over 26 were much less inclined to have been involved in criminal activities before their heroin use than were those under 26. This again is an important finding.

SEXUAL DEVIANCE

One of my very first impressions of female addicts, as I interviewed them in Manhattan Rehabilitation Center, was that there were a number of rather obvious lesbians. In terms of the incidence of female homosexuality, Manhattan Rehabilitation Center is much more like a women's prison (as described in David Ward and Gene Kassenbaum's book *Women's Prison: Sex and the Social Structure*)[8] than a therapeutic community on the order of Synanon[9] or New York's Phoenix Houses.[10] Homosexual behavior at Manhattan Rehabilitation Center is more the norm than the exception; liaisons are established by almost everyone who enters the center, whether she is lesbian on the outside or not. In many ways, much of this activity is a way of overcoming both the general malaise of being locked up in a dull institution and the general boredom that pervades the whole center.

Despite the fact that many women addicts participate in homosexual activity only while they are in institutions such as Manhattan Rehabilitation Center, a good number participated in homosexual relations before they actually used heroin. In response to the question:

> On the outside, before you used heroin, did you primarily have sex with women or with men or was it about half and half?

Twenty-nine percent of the women in our first female sample of 70 said they had primarily homosexual or bisexual relations, while only 3% of 224 men reported this sexual behavior. Even if there was a considerable under-reporting, as we would expect from our male sample—male homosexuality is much more of a stigma in our society than is female homosexuality and thus is less likely to be admitted in interviews such as ours—the difference between the sexes was considerable.

Surprisingly, the percentages of males and females admitting homosexuality after heroin use does not change to any significant degree. When we asked the same question about behavior after using heroin, 28% of the females reported homosexual or bisexual activity, while 4% of the males did. Generally with heroin use and subsequent adoption of a deviant career there is a general loosening of attitudes and behavior about sexual activity. A large number of female addicts are forced at some time or another in their careers

8. David Ward and Gene Kassenbaum *Women's Prison: Sex and the Social Structure* (Chicago: Aldine Publishing Company, 1965).
9. Lewis Yablonsky: *Synanon: The Tunnel Back* (New York: The Macmillan Company, 1967); and Dan Casriel, *So Fair a House: The Story of Synanon* (Englewood Cliffs, N.J.: Prentice-Hall, Inc., 1963).
10. George Nash, "The Sociology of Phoenix House—A Therapeutic Community for the Resocialization of Narcotic Addicts" (mimeographed, Columbia University Bureau of Applied Social Research, 1969).

to resort to prostitution to earn money to support their need for drugs. Having once resorted to prostitution a woman's attitude about sex becomes less sacred. Sex becomes a way of earning money, as well as an expression of love or an activity for pleasure. Indeed for some both the drive for sex and its pleasurable sensations are dulled and thwarted while they use heroin.

Age is associated with homosexual and bisexual activity before heroin use, most particularly with those in our sample over 21 years of age. Of the youngest group of women, those under 21 years of age, 18% reported homosexual and bisexual activity before heroin use, while 42% of those from 21 to 26 years of age and 29% of those over 26 reported it. These findings seem to support our general impression that younger addicts are less pathological, exhibit fewer neurotic or psychological symptoms, and use drugs more because of their social significance than their older counterparts.

GOING TO TREATMENT

In some respects it is far easier for women to support their addiction than it is for men. Women have a ready commodity to sell —themselves. Even the most ugly and physically run down women addicts can somehow manage to turn enough tricks to support themselves. If they are young or beautiful they may easily support another addict or pimp as well. Marie, whom I mentioned earlier in chapter 3, was young and not particularly pretty, but she regularly supported her pimp and on occasion a second male. Mary Terry, a very beautiful ex-addict staff member at New York's Phoenix House, summed up the ease with which women can hustle with candor in a tape-recording that was transcribed in the Phoenix House publication, *Reach Out*:

> I feel it's a lot easier for women to make it in the streets than men. They have a commodity that will sell when money won't. There's always somebody in the market for that, for a piece, to put it really where it's at. A girl can always go out and make five dollars for a bag with less jeopardy than a guy, with less fear of being busted or arrested.[11]

Police in New York are reluctant to arrest prostitutes except when prostitution becomes too obvious and political pressures force them to make one of their periodic clean-ups. Judges are equally

11. Phoenix House Foundation, *Reach Out*, Vol. 1, no. 2 (1970).

reluctant to convict them. When they are convicted the sentences are usually short ones.

One of the consequences of this apparent ease with which women can support themselves is that they tend to go to treatment facilities far less often than do male addicts. Only one in four (20%) said that she had previously stayed overnight in treatment, while more than two out of five males (43%) had been in previous treatment. Furthermore, men, when they go into treatment, go more frequently than women do. Of those women who had been in treatment, only 5% had had more than two previous stays as compared to 14% of the males. As women can support themselves more easily than men, they feel less pressure to go into treatment or to "clean up" in detoxification.

PAYING DUES

Certainly at some levels it is easier for women to hustle, but they seem to suffer from their addiction and its concomitant life more than men do. The female ex-addict staff members of Phoenix Houses are particularly aware of the problems of women addicts vis-à-vis men and society in general while using, in the street, in treatment, and even after successful treatment when they give up drugs and assume stable, productive lives. Rae Dibble, now director of a Phoenix House, described the problems of women in Phoenix Houses:

> In the business of making it in a therapeutic community, I think that women, because of some of the standards of society, like the fallen woman have a much harder time. She does so many things [while an addict] that are frowned upon. I don't know why that is —I don't agree with it. But I think a woman who has hit the gutter and done some things as a drug user has a large residual guilt about it. Not to say that men don't. But because society stereotypes women. I think that in making it back they have this on some kind of unconscious level to deal with.

Even women who are long drug free and living radically different lives than they had as addicts suffer pangs of remorse and guilt about their past behavior as addicts. Another Puerto Rican woman at Phoenix House who had worked her way up through the program as a paid staff member to become Assistant Director said this when I talked to her about this problem:

Sometimes I still feel as if I'm somehow tainted, being unworthy of men and society. I did the whole bit on the street. I hustled and lived with other women, but that was long ago and I'm another person now. I can't understand why I feel this way, but I do. I guess women fall harder when they fall.

I do not think that one can explain these problems of women on the grounds of mental illness. Women addicts are not necessarily more mentally ill than men. Dr. Carl Chambers, who is now head of the research section of New York's Narcotic Addiction Control Commission and who has done considerable research with women addicts, in 1967 compared psychiatric diagnoses of 43 men and 54 women at Lexington Hospital and found no differences in concurrent diagnosis for the two groups.[12] In fact, if anything males were more often diagnosed as having personality pattern disorders (11, or 26%, did) than were females (2, or 4%, did). Yet women seem to suffer or express their suffering more than men do.

If indeed women do suffer their addiction and its associated behavior more than men it may be because of the ways that roles are defined among the sexes:

It's all right for a man to go around and be a pimp, if need be, to have very loose, easy sexual relationships. There's nothing wrong with that. Society's always said that's all right. In fact its tied up with proving your masculinity. But, if you're a woman the stereotype thing as a woman is the pure one who awaits the great love of her life.[13]

A male can become addicted, "rip off" everyone around him, turn his "old lady" or wife out into the streets to hustle, and feel less remorse and guilt than a woman who does the same thing. This behavior, while despised by society, is accepted as possible for a male. Some persons even appear to romanticize such actions. In some ways it is seen to be more manly for a man to have experienced some such transgressions against society.

This is not the case for women; they, as the quote above says, "fall harder when they fall." Women do not bounce back as easily after their addiction as do men, and society does not accept them back as readily because it does not allow them to "sin." When they do, they feel the stigma so strongly that it is still felt long after a woman changes her life, which suggests that perhaps society does not allow women the redemption after sin that it allows men.

There are, I think, several reasons for this. American society

12. From a personal communication with Dr. Chambers.
13. Quote from Pauline Kaufman, "square" staff, in Phoenix House, *Reach Out*, Vol. 1, no. 2 (1970).

stigmatizes addicts, prostitutes, and homosexuals and often the female addict is at least two of them—sometimes three. Let us start with prostitution. Although prostitution may be an easy way to get ready money it brings with it a certain indignity. Prostitution is a much more personal action than theft, burglary, or drug sales, the usual male hustles. You give more of yourself when you give your body. During a burglary, the burglar need not necessarily confront the person he is stealing from; if he does he has bungled the job. In a theft, the confrontation is most often only for a short time, a matter of seconds or at the most a few minutes. You can detach yourself from the person you steal from if you do not have to see him for more than a fleeting moment. Prostitution takes more time and is more intimate. However a woman may steel herself to this intimacy, you have to deal with a man when he uses your body. Prostitutes attempt to overcome this enforced intimacy by using the concepts of "Johns" and "tricks":

> I never respond to them physically; they're only tricks. You don't think nothing about no tricks, however they look or nice they are. You try to take whatever is personal out of it—make it like business.

Despite their attempts to steel themselves to the situation, any continuing prostitution forces women to deal with society's prescription of feminine behavior:

> A girl has it easier making the dollar but harder paying some personal dues, because she's so hard on herself. And, God knows, she has all the kinds of ideals about a woman, too, and she falls so short of these as a dope fiend woman.[14]

In matters of sex, despite the mass media's sexual revolution (it surely didn't get to the persons in our sample), women are expected to be fairly exclusive. Girls as they are growing up suppress their sexuality until they meet the "one man" who will give them "fulfillment." Women are expected to wait until they love or like someone. These attitudes are particularly strong among working-class groups. Prostitutes are definitely not exclusive, and society stigmatizes them for abandoning its model of proper behavior for women. Prostitutes suffer from this stigma with considerable guilt and remorse.

Often they grow to dislike men and scorn "square" society, and maybe they are justified in doing this. They are often treated very badly by "tricks" and are subject to a variety of inflicted perversions.

14. Rae Dibble, *Reach Out*, Vol. 1, no. 2 (1970).

Men often feel that the price of a prostitute justifies any indignity. Women have to be continually on the lookout for:

> . . . fucking freaks; you don't know what some of these guys will do. You got to stay awake, keep your wits; if you get too loose you'll get your ass torn or somebody will beat the shit out of you.

Is it any wonder they become cynical and skeptical about men.

Society does no better by them; its ambivalence is obvious. Prostitution is accepted as necessary, but prostitutes are stigmatized. The law and law-enforcement agencies express this precisely: the prostitute can be arrested and charged but the John is let go.

As one might expect, many women addicts go to other women for what love and sexual satisfaction they can get. Some become active and obvious lesbians, which brings with it still another stigma. Rae Dibble described this multiple stigma and the problems that women face overcoming it:

> They've been ex-prostitutes, they've been ex-convicts, ex-lesbians, ex-thieves [and one may add ex-addicts]. You know it's one stigma after another. . . . But I know from my own experience that it's much harder for women to overcome it than men.

The current women's liberation movement says that it is enough just to be a woman, that society oppresses them by defining the role of women in narrow constricting ways. Perhaps they are correct, but the "normal" woman's burden is light compared to that of the woman addict who is usually at once a woman, an addict, a prostitute, a convict, and, in some instances, a lesbian.

But there is also another way to view this. Yes, society's definition of femininity does deny women certain freedoms that some now wish to regain, but there are also certain residual, oblique advantages to the narrower limits of behavior expected of women. I am sure it is the restricting definition of femininity and society's pressure to restrain the freedom of women that have contained the numbers of "criminal addicts" among women in the United States.

Before the Harrison Act of 1914 women made up by far the majority of addicts; today men outnumber women approximately four to one. This dramatic shift in the addict population occurred because the Harrison Act and subsequent court decisions criminalized narcotic addicts. While it was not a crime to be an addict, it became a crime to possess opiates or the paraphernalia to use them —which amounts to the same thing. Prior to the Harrison Act addicts were not considered criminal, as Marie Nyswander wrote in her book, *The Drug Addict as Patient*:

It is important at this juncture to realize that the drug addict before 1914 had little or no involvement with criminal activity. He carried on his job, maintained his home and family life. His illness did not inflict injury on any one other than himself. He considered himself and was considered by others to be grappling with a definite and difficult problem and he expected to obtain treatment in a legitimate manner.[15]

In subsequent years they have been defined and treated as criminals.

Women as a group are socialized more effectively in our society than men (pressured, if you like) and feel more constraint to abide by laws and mores, and when addiction was criminalized by the laws far fewer women became involved. Men, on the other hand, are given more freedom and are socialized less effectively; they transgress laws and mores more in nearly every respect. Women were deterred by the criminalization of addiction; men were not and became the majority of addicts. Today when women become addicts they suffer more guilt and remorse because it is harder for them to go against society's prescription for femininity and its laws and mores.

15. Marie Nyswander, *The Drug Addict as Patient* (New York and London: Grune and Stratton, Inc., 1956).

Bibliography

Aronowitz, Dennis S. "Civil Commitment." In *Task Force Report: Narcotics and Drug Abuse.* President's Commission on Law Enforcement and Administration of Justice, 1967.

Ball, John C. "Two Patterns of Narcotic Drug Addiction in the United States." In *The International Journal of the Addictions,* Vol. 56, no. 1 (1965).

Becker, Howard, ed. *Outsiders.* Glencoe, Ill.: The Free Press, 1963.

————. *The Other Side: Perspectives on Deviance.* Glencoe, Ill.: The Free Press, 1964.

Blake, James. *The Joint.* New York: Doubleday & Company, Inc., 1971.

Blum, Richard H., and associates. *Drugs I: Society and Drugs.* San Francisco: Jossey-Bass, Inc., 1969.

————. *Drugs II: Students and Drugs.* San Francisco: Jossey-Bass, Inc., 1969.

Brill, Henry, and Larimore, Granville W. "Second On-Site Study of the British Narcotic System." In *N.A.C.C. Reprints,* Vol. 1, no. 2 (1965).

Brown, Claude. *Manchild in the Promised Land.* New York: The Macmillan Company, 1965.

Burroughs, William. *Junkie.* Ace Books, Inc., 1953. Originally published under the pseudonym William Lee.

————. *Naked Lunch.* New York: Grove Press, Inc., 1966.

————. *Nova Express.* London: Jonathan Cape Ltd., 1966.

178

Casriel, Daniel Harold. *So Fair a House: The Story of Synanon.* Englewood Cliffs, N.J.: Prentice-Hall, Inc., 1963.

Chambers, Carl D., Hinesley, R., and Moldestad, Mary. "Narcotic Addiction in Females: A Race Comparison." In *The International Journal of the Addictions,* Vol. 5, no. 1 (1970).

———, Moffett, Arthur D., and Jones, Judith P. "Demographic Factors Associated with Negro Opiate Addiction." In *The International Journal of the Addictions,* Vol. 3, no. 3 (1968).

Chein, Isidor. "Psychological Functions of Drug Use." Paper read at Symposium on the Scientific Basis of Drug Dependence, 8–9 April 1968, London.

———. "Psychological, Social and Epidemiological Factors in Drug Addiction." In *Rehabilitating the Narcotic Addict.* Washington, D.C.: U.S. Government Printing Office, 1967.

———; Gerard, Donald L.; Lee, Robert S.; and Rosenberg, Eva. *The Road to H.* New York: Basic Books, Inc., 1964.

Clark, Kenneth B. *Dark Ghetto: Dilemmas of Social Power.* New York: Harper & Row, Publishers, 1965.

Clausen, John A. "Drug Addiction." In Merton and Nisbet, eds., *Contemporary Social Problems,* 2nd ed. New York: Harcourt Brace Jovanovich, Inc., 1966.

Dai, Bingham. *Opiate Addiction in Chicago.* Shanghai: The Commercial Press, 1937.

Dole, Vincent P., and Nyswander, Marie E. "Successful Treatment of 750 Criminal Addicts." In *The Journal of the American Medical Association,* Vol. 206 (1968).

Duval, Henrietta J., Locke, Ben, and Brill, Leon. "Follow-up Study of Addicts Five Years after Hospitalization." In *Public Health Reports,* Vol. 98, no. 3 (1963).

Eldridge, William Butler. *Narcotics and the Law.* American Bar Association. New York: New York University Press, 1962.

Ellinwood, E. H., Smith, W. G., and Vaillant, G. E. "Narcotic Addiction in Males and Females: A Comparison." In *The International Journal of the Addictions,* Vol. 1, no. 2 (1966).

Fort, Joel. *The Pleasure Seekers: The Drug Crisis, Youth and Society.* New York: Grove Press, Inc., 1970.

Gearing, Frances R. "Evaluation of Methadone Mantenance Treatment Program: Progress Report through October 3, 1968." Mimeographed, Columbia University School of Public Health and Administrative Medicine, 1968.

———. "Evaluation of Methadone Maintenance Treatment Program: Progress Report through March 31, 1969." Mimeographed, Columbia University School of Public Health and Administrative Medicine, 1969.

†Glaser, Frederick B. "Misinformation About Drugs: A Problem for Drug Abuse Education." In *The International Journal of the Addictions*, Vol. 5, no. 1 (1970).

———. "Narcotic Addiction in the Pain-Prone Female Patient." In *The International Journal of the Addictions*, Vol. 1, no. 2 (1966).

Goffman, Erving. *Asylums*. Garden City, N.Y.: Doubleday & Company, Inc., 1961.

Goode, Erich. "The Marijuana Market." In *Columbia University Forum*, Vol. 12, no. 4 (1969).

Goode, William J. "Family Disorganization." In Merton and Nisbet, eds., *Contemporary Social Problems*. New York: Harcourt Brace Jovanovich, Inc., 1961.

Hall, Margaret E. "Mental and Physical Efficiency of Women Drug Addicts." In *The Journal of Abnormal and Social Psychiatry*, Vol. 33 (1938).

Halpern, Milton, and Rho, Yong-Myun. "Deaths from Narcotism in New York City." In *The International Journal of the Addictions*, Vol. 2, no. 1 (1967).

Harris, John D. *The Junkie Priest: Father Daniel Egan, S.A.* New York: Coward-McCann, Inc., 1964.

Hawks, D. V. "The Dimensions of Drug Dependence in the United Kingdom." In *The International Journal of the Addictions*, Vol. 6, no. 1 (1971).

Hentoff, Nat. *A Doctor among the Addicts*. New York: Grove Press, Inc., 1968.

Hirsch, Phil, ed. *Hooked*. New York: Pyramid Publications, 1968.

Hughes, Helen MacGill, ed. *The Fantastic Lodge*. Greenwich, Conn.: Fawcett World Library, Premier Books, 1971.

Irwin, John. *The Felon*. Englewood Cliffs, N.J.: Prentice-Hall, Inc., 1970.

Joseph, Herman. "Heroin Addiction and Methadone Maintenance." Mimeographed, Metropolitan Urban Services Training Facility, New York, 1968.

Kaplan, John. *Marijuana: The New Prohibition*. World Publishing Company, 1970.

Kim, Susan I. "Narcotic Addiction: A Comparative Study of Eight Countries." Mimeographed, Columbia University Bureau of Applied Social Research, New York, 1968.

King, Alexander. *Mine Enemy Grows Older*. New York: Simon & Schuster, Inc., 1958.

La Motte, Ellen N. *The Ethics of Opium*. New York and London: The Century Company, 1924.

Langrod, John. "Secondary Drug Use among Heroin Users." In *The International Journal of the Addictions*, Vol. 5, no. 4 (1970).

Larner, Jeremy, and Tefferteller, Ralph. *The Addict in the Street*. New York: Grove Press, Inc., 1964.

Lennard, Henry L., and associates. *Mystification and Drug Misuse*. San Francisco: Jossey-Bass, Inc., 1971.

Lindesmith, Alfred. *The Addict and the Law*. Bloomington, Ind.: Indiana University Press, 1965.

———. "Dope Fiend Mythology." In *Journal of Criminal Law and Criminology*, Vol. 31 (1940).

———. *Opiate Addiction*. Bloomington, Ind.: Principia Press, 1947.

Lipton, Robert Jay. *Thought Reform and the Psychology of Totalism: A Study of Brainwashing in China*. New York: W. W. Norton & Company, Inc., 1961.

Malitz, S. "Psychopharmacology: A Cultural Approach." In *Symposium: Non-Narcotic Drug Dependency and Addiction*, Proceedings of the New York County District Branch, American Psychiatric Association, March 10, 1966.

May, Edgar. "Drugs Without Crime: A Report on the British Success with Heroin Addiction." In *Harpers Magazine*, July 1971.

Nash, George. "The Sociology of Phoenix House." Mimeographed, Columbia University Bureau of Applied Social Research, New York, 1969.

——— and Cohen, Eli. "An Analysis of New York City Police Statistics for Narcotic Arrests during the Period 1957–1967." Mimeographed, Columbia University Bureau of Applied Social Research, New York, 1969.

———; Waldorf, Dan; Foster, Kay; and Kyllingstad, Ann. "The Phoenix House Program: The Results of a Two-Year Follow-up." Mimeographed, 1971.

New York State Narcotic Addiction Control Commission. *Report . . . the First Twenty-one-Month Period: April 1, 1967, through December 31, 1968*.

Nyswander, Marie E. *The Drug Addict as Patient*. New York and London: Grune and Stratton, Inc., 1956.

O'Donnell, John. *Narcotic Addicts in Kentucky*. Washington, D.C.: U.S. Government Printing Office, 1970.

Parry, Hugh J. "Use of Psychotropic Drugs by U.S. Adults." In *Public Health Reports*, Vol. 83 (1968).

Perkins, Marvin E., and Bloch, Harriet. "A Study of Some Failures in Methadone Treatment." Paper read at the 123rd Annual Meeting of the American Psychiatric Association, 11–15 May 1970, San Francisco.

Pescor, M. "A Comparative Statistical Study of Male and Female Drug Addicts." In *American Journal of Psychiatry*, Vol. 100 (1944).

Phoenix House Foundation. *Reach Out*, Vol. 1, no. 2 (1970).

Polsky, Ned. *Hustlers, Beats and Others*. Chicago: Aldine Publishing Company, 1967.

Preble, Edward, and Casey, John H. "Taking Care of Business—The Heroin User's Life on the Street." In *The International Journal of the Addictions*, Vol. 4, no. 1 (1969).

Proctor, Mac. "The Habit." In *The International Journal of the Addictions*, Vol. 6, no. 1 (1971).

Rado, S. "Fighting Narcotic Bondage and Other Forms of Narcotic Disorders." In *Comprehensive Psychiatry*, Vol. 4, no. 3 (1963).

Robins, Lee. "Drug Use in a Normal Population of Young Negro Men." In *American Journal of Public Health*, Vol. 57, no. 9 (1967).

Rosenblum, Constance. "Face to Face: An Interview with Mary Terry, Rae Dibble, and Pauline Kaufman." In *Reach Out* (New York, Friends of Phoenix House), Vol. 1, no. 2 (1970).

Rubington, Earl. "Drug Addiction as a Deviant Career." In *The International Journal of the Addictions*, Vol. 2, no. 1 (1967).

Schmidt, J. E. *Narcotics Lingo and Lore*. Springfield, Ill.: Charles C. Thomas, Publisher, 1959.

Schofield, Michael. *The Strange Case of Pot*. Harmondsworth, England: Penguin Books, 1971.

Scott, J. M. *The White Poppy*. New York: Funk and Wagnalls, 1969.

Spira, Joseph, Ball, John C., and Cottrell, Emily S. "Addictions to Methadone Among Patients at Lexington and Ft. Worth." In *Public Health Reports*, Vol. 83, no. 8 (1968).

Stern, Bill, and Fraley, Oscar. *The Taste of Ashes*. New York: Henry Holt and Company, 1959.

Thomas, Piri. *Down These Mean Streets*. New York: Alfred A. Knopf, Inc., 1967.

Trocchi, Alexander. *Cain's Book*. New York: Grove Press, Inc., 1960.

Trussell, Ray E. "Treatment of Narcotic Addicts in New York City." In *The International Journal of the Addictions*, Vol. 5, no. 3 (1970).

Vaillant, George E. "A Twelve-Year Follow-Up of New York Narcotic Addicts: I. The Relation of Treatment to Outcome." In *The American Journal of Psychiatry*, Vol. 122, no. 7 (1966).

———. "A Twelve-Year Follow-Up of New York Narcotic Addicts: IV. Some Characteristics and Determinants of Abstinence." In *The American Journal of Psychiatry*, Vol. 123 (1966).

Volkman, Rita, and Cressey, Donald R. "Differential Association and Rehabilitation of Drug Addicts." In *American Journal of Sociology*, Vol. 69 (1963).

Wakefield, Dan, ed. *The Addict*. New York: Fawcett World Library, 1963.

Waldorf, Dan. "Life without Heroin: Some Social Adjustments during Long-Term Periods of Voluntary Abstention." In *Social Problems*, Fall 1970.

———. "Social Control in Therapeutic Communities for Treatment of Drug Addicts." In *The International Journal of the Addictions*, Vol. 6, no. 1 (1971).

Ward, David, and Kassebaum, Gene. *Women's Prison: Sex and the Social Structure*. Chicago: Aldine Publishing Company, 1965.

Weissman, Sidney. "The Significance of Diagnosis in Treatment of Narcotic Addicts." In *The International Journal of the Addictions*, Vol. 5, no. 4 (1970).

Winick, Charles. "Maturing Out of Narcotic Addiction." In *U.N. Bulletin on Narcotics*, Vol. 14 (1962).

———. "Physician Addicts." In *Social Problems*, Fall 1963.

Yablonsky, Lewis. *Synanon: the Tunnel Back*. New York: The Macmillan Company, 1965.

Zimmering, Paul; Toolan, James; Safrin, Ranate; and Wortis, Bernard S. "Heroin Addiction in Adolescent Boys." In *Journal of Nervous and Mental Disease*, Vol. 114 (1951).

Index

184